U0039011

9789575472115

CHANG PING-LIN (1869-1936):

A POLITICAL RADICAL AND CULTURAL CONSERVATIVE

by

Jer-shiarn Lee

The Liberal Arts Press

2

國立中央圖書館出版品預行編目資料

Chang Ping-Lin (1869-1936) : a political
radical and cultural conservative = 章炳
麟(一八六九 - 一九三六) : 一位政治激進主
義者及文化保守主義者 / 李哲賢著. -- 初版
.-- 臺北市 : 文史哲, 民82
  面 ; 公分
參考書目:面
ISBN 957-547-211-X(平裝)

1. 章炳麟 - 傳記

782.882   82002631

CHANG PING-LIN (1869-1936): A POLITICAL

RADICAL AND CULTURAL CONSERVATIVE

章炳麟（一八六九～一九三六）：
一位政治激進主義者及文化保守主義者

著　　者：李　　哲　　賢
出 版 者：文　史　哲　出　版　社
登記證字號：行政院新聞局局版臺業字第五三三七號
發 行 所：文　史　哲　出　版　社
印 刷 者：文　史　哲　出　版　社
　　　臺北市羅斯福路一段七十二巷四號
　郵　撥：○五一二八八一二彭正雄帳戶
　電　話：三　五　一　一　○　二　八
定價新臺幣三○○元

中 華 民 國 八 十 二 年 四 月 初 版

CHANG PING-LIN (1869-1936):

A POLITICAL RADICAL AND CULTURAL CONSERVATIVE

by

Jer-shiarn Lee

4

To My Parents,

My Beloved Wife

and Two Children

ACKNOWLEDGEMENTS

I became engaged in the study of Chang Ping-lin and his core idea, the preservation of the national essence, in 1986 when I took a seminar course supervised by Professor Charles Hedtke, my dissertation director. I read a great number of documents concerning the life and thought of the subject. I have also greatly benefitted by the Western Conference of the Association for Asian Studies held at the University of Arizona on October 30-31, 1987, which provided me with an opportunity to present my findings on the subject. From the above, I could formulate the theme of my study of Chang Ping-lin, who had not been considered by modern scholars and historians.

I am grateful to all those who have assisted me in the completion of this work . First of all, I would like to thank my dissertation committee. Professor Charles Hedtke was very kind to take the responsibility as my dissertation director after Professor William Schultz retired. I am deeply indebted to Professor Hedtke, for his inspiration, encouragement and valuable advice on the research and writing. Without his inspiring and encouraging support, I could not have completed my book this year. Also, his assistance in improving both the content and style contributed greatly to the completion o f the book in its present form.

Professor William Schultz kindly read the first chapter of my book and improved its content and writing. He also provided invaluable insight into the problems of Chinese intellectual history. I owe much gratitude to Professor Jing-shen Tao, for his invaluable advice on this study and his moral encouragement and support in many ways. Professor Robert Gimello also offered many critical suggestions in improving the quality of this work.

I also wish to thank Mrs. Deirdre Campbell, a former librarian at the Arid Lands Library, who kindly and patiently helped me type all the manuscripts of my book. Her assistance and friendship are invaluable.

Finally, I wish to express my special gratitude to my wife, Yu-mei Wu, for encouragement and support during the years of my study in the United States, and for her writing the Chinese characters in this work.

TABLE OF CONTENTS

ABBREVIATION USED IN THE NOTES

BDRC   <u>Biographical Dictionary of Republican China</u> (by Howard Boorman).

CLHC   <u>Chang T'ai-yen cheng-lun hsüan-chi</u> (ed. by T'ang Chih-chün).

CSTS   <u>Chang-shih ts'ung-shu</u>.

CTYCC   <u>Chang Tai-yen ch'üan-chi</u>.

ECCP   <u>Eminent Chinese of the Ch'ing Period</u> (ed. by Arthur Hummel).

NPCP   <u>Chang Tai-yen nien-p'u ch'ang-pien</u> (by Tang Chih-chün).

TTNP   <u>Tai-yen hsien-sheng tzu-ting nien-p'u</u> (by Chang Ping-lin).

ABSTRACT

Although Chang Ping-lin is well-known for his role in the revolutionary movement that culminated in the termination of imperial rule in 1911, he is more often remembered as a prominent classical scholar. His life and thought illustrates the uneasy relationship between political revolution and cultural conservatism among the intellectuals of his generation, and his advocacy of preserving the national essence paved the way for the far-reaching National Essence Movement in the early twentieth century. This dissertation, thus, represents a study of the tension between politics and culture among Chinese intellectuals and the significance of cultural conservatism during that era.

Chang's concern to preserve the national essence was not only because he was a classical scholar, and therefor, felt a responsibility to uphold classical teachings, but also because he believed it was essential for the survival of the nation. Under pressure from Western powers, Chang was afraid that Chinese culture was threatened with extinction. In order to prevent foreign conquest, Chang believed that reform or revolution in China was necessary, and that the most important mission of the reformer or revolutionary was to preserve her unique culture. Therefor, he gave priority to the preservation of the national essence over that of the nation. The latter was important only because it was needed to save the former. And reform or revolution was in turn necessary to save the nation.

Chang's lifelong commitment to the preservation of the national essence manifested itself in his two careers: one as a political activist and the other as a classical scholar. Even after the establishment of the Republic of China, Chang remained active in the political arena. He continued to speak out against whatever he perceived to endanger China's sovereignty or its culture. Apart from his involvement in politics, Chang also devoted himself to teaching and the study of China's rich cultural heritage. This effort to preserve the national essence was the most consistent thread in his life.

章炳麟（一八六九～一九三六）：
一位政治激進主義者及文化保守主義者

前　言

　　本書主要在於探究章炳麟先生之生平與思想，特別是他對保存國粹之關切及此種關切與其參與辛亥革命之關連。章氏一生正反映出當時知識分子中，政治革命論與文化保守主義間那種尖銳而不安之關係。本書之所以以章氏作為研究之對象，部分乃因為章氏在近代中國思想史上扮演一個極其重要之角色。然而，更重要的理由是，雖然章氏是近代中國史上一位主要之思想家、學者及政治行動家，在西方之學術界中，有關章氏研究之著作卻是屈指可數。在近代中國思想研究方面，章氏之所以受到普遍的忽視，其實是有其理由的。

　　由於章氏行文之風格出自魏、晉，文字過於艱深古雅，加之其思想又深受西方及本土思想之多重影響，凡此皆足以使其著作令人難以理解。另一原因是，章氏之思想並不適用於「保守或激進」之分析範疇。此種範疇乃是現代歷史學者用來探究近代中國知識分子之思想的一種解釋性設計。雖然，作為一種解釋性之範疇，「保守或激進」此一區分有其解釋上或分析上之效用；然而，用來分析像章氏此一類型之思想家卻並不適用。蓋章氏雖然可稱之為保守主義者，或更精確地說，他是一位文化保守主義者；可是，在政治或政治革命之領域裡，章氏同時也是一位激進主義者。

　　即使在西方之學術界，有關章氏研究之有數著作中，對於章氏生平與思想之評估亦無法令人滿意，其中之一個觀點是，章氏之思想本身充滿著矛盾。章氏曾經是康、梁改革派之擁護者，其後卻投入革命之陣營；作為一個革命分子，他卻提倡國粹不遺餘力；他是一位國學家，卻又對儒學加以抨擊；更有進者，章氏雖提倡共和政體，卻譴責代議政治。然而，這些矛盾之外觀，大部分是可以消滅或甚而解消的。只要吾人了解此乃出自於章氏致力於保存國粹之結果；而保存國粹之努力又是章氏一生之思想脈絡中最首尾一貫的。因為，對章氏本人而言，所有這些表面上呈現矛盾紛紜之觀念，卻只是達成其保存國粹此一終極目的之手段而已。因此，章氏本人在政治立場或觀點上之改變，從章氏保存國粹之關切此一角度看來，就一點也並不矛盾了。由於保存國粹乃是章氏思想中之核心觀念及最基本且恒常之特質。因此，對於章氏生平與思想之研究當呈顯其思想中之此一層面。遺憾的是，在章氏思想之研究方面，中、西學者皆普遍忽略其思想中之此一核心觀念，也因此局限了吾人對於章氏思想之理解。因此，對章氏之思想再加以評估也就有強烈之必要了。作者希望此一研究章氏一生之英文著作能對章氏之生平及思想之進一步了解有所裨益。

　　這是一本完整研究章炳麟此一思想家之英文著作。作者參閱所有盡可能搜集得到之有關章氏之中文及英文的第一手及第二手之研究資料。本書主要在於探究章炳麟此一著名之國學家及政治行動家之生平與思想。本書並非有關章氏之思想傳記，而是以思想史之方法來研究章氏。本書乃是以章氏之生平與思想作為基點來探究清末及民初中國思想之變遷。章氏之思想反映了此一時期一個重要而迄今尚未為人所研究之思想層面。章氏之生平與思想呈示出他那一代之知識分子中政治及文化理想間所產生之張力。並且，章氏終生對於保存國粹此一理念之執著，預示了近代中國思想史中最重要的思潮之一的國粹運動。此種文化保守主義在反抗民初主張全盤西化之運動中，扮演了一個非常重要之角色。甚而，新文化運動之興起亦是針對此一國粹派之文化保守主義而來。因此，作者相信，根據中、英文之相關資料來分析章氏之生平與思想，將有助於對章氏之生平與思想獲致一較佳之理解。並且，對於此一時期之政治激進主義與文化保守主義間之關係以及文化保守主義在近代中國思想史中所扮演之角色，皆將會有一新的視野。

雖然章炳麟在辛亥革命運動中極其有名；然而，身爲國學家的他卻因之而更享盛名。章氏之生平與思想反映了他那一世代之知識分子中，政治革命論與文化保守主義間那種不安之關係；並且，章氏對於保存國粹之鼓吹更爲二十世紀初期影響深遠之國粹運動鋪路。本書旨在以章氏之生平與思想作爲基點，來探究二十世紀初期之中國知識分子中，文化與政治間之張力及文化保守主義此一思潮之重要性。

章氏對於保存國粹之關切，並不只是因爲他是一位國學家；因而，深覺有擁護傳統學術之責任；而且，更是因爲他相信保存國粹對於一個國家民族之存亡有其必要性。由於西力之入侵，章氏深恐本國文化受到西方文化之威脅而滅亡。爲了免於中國爲外人所征服，章氏相信，改革或革命對中國而言是有其必要的；並且，改革家或革命家最重要之使命即在於維護傳統文化於不墜。因此，章氏視保存國粹比保衛國家本身更具有優先性；而保護國家之所以重要，只是因爲它對保存國粹而言是有其必要的。而改革或革命對救國而言，相對的，亦是必要的。

作爲一位革命家，章氏卻要求維護國粹。章氏之注重國粹保存，使他明顯地有別於參與革命運動中之其他知識分子。因爲，對當時大部分之知識分子而言，他們所關心的並非傳統文化之維護，而是爲了保衛國家此一政治實體。雖然，章氏亦關心國家之存亡；但對章氏本人而言，國家並不僅僅是一政治實體而已；而且更是一文化實體。因之，章氏雖然仍舊關心國家富強之追求；然而，章氏之終極關切或目的卻是爲了使傳統文化不因外力之入侵而亡滅。甚至當章氏主編民報——同盟會之機關報——時，章氏把民報從一份通俗而激進之機關報變為幾乎像國粹學報那麼學術性之刊物。章氏後來並且捲入國粹運動此一文化保守主義之運動中。此種文化保守主義乃是近代中國思想史中最重要之思潮之一，其後且受到五四運動中之反傳統激進主義之挑激。

章氏一生對保存國粹之執著，明顯地表現於他兩種不同之生涯中：一個是政治行動家；而另一個卻是國學家。民國建立之後，章氏在政治舞臺上仍舊十分活躍；章氏並繼續抨擊任何足以危及中國之主權與文化之行動或個人。除了參與政治之外，章氏並獻身於傳統學術文化之教學與研究。因之，致力於國粹之保存乃是章氏一生中最前後一貫之思想脈絡。

本書共分七章。

第一章：「導論」。

第二章：「章氏之早年生活及其思想背景」。一八九五年當章氏開始參與政治之時，他已經承受了包括來自本土及外來思想之廣泛影響。其中，漢學形成其學術之基礎。蓋漢學擴大章氏之學術興趣；特別是關於中國傳統文化方面。

第三章：「章氏與國粹」。此章分析章氏之國粹概念及其範圍與意義。「國粹」一詞乃是借自日本之新詞語。章氏對國粹保存之主張，不僅僅是出自於其對西力衝擊之反應所產生之文化認同上之焦慮感而已。因為，作為一位國學家，章氏非常明白保存國粹對國家存亡所具之重要性此一事實。章氏對接受國粹之態度，並非是全盤且毫無保留地接受中國之傳統文化。因為，章氏之接納中國文化乃是具批判性的；並且，他非常清楚中國文化中之那些成分是應當加以保留的。因此，章氏接受國粹之態度是極其審慎的。對章氏而言，國粹意指中國歷史及文化傳統特質中，那些仍舊適用於現代中國之成分或要素。

第四章：「章氏邁向革命之路」。此章分析章氏一八九五年至一九一一年間參與政治之活動及促使章氏之政治立場由改革轉向革命之緣由。章氏自一八九五年以來即是革新分子。自中國在中日甲午戰爭中慘敗後，章氏即相信，要拯救中國必須提倡改革。然而，章氏支持康、梁的革新運動之真意乃是基於他對保存國粹之關切。因為，章氏認為國家之生存乃是使國粹不亡之不二法門。章氏之立場之由改革轉向革命乃是由於一九〇〇年所發生之義和團事件。此一事件使中國產生極大之危機。但因滿清政府無力抵抗外力之入侵，章氏乃訴諸革命以救國。然而，對章氏而言，革命亦只是達成其保存國粹此一終極目的之手段而已。

第五章：「章氏在民國時期之活動」。在民國時期，章氏在政治上仍極其活躍。除了政治活動外，章氏則埋首於傳統學術之研究。一九一一年以後，章氏發行了「華國」月刊及「制言」半月刊此兩種刊物，且創辦「國學講習會」，經由這些媒介，章氏致力於中國傳統文化之保存與發揚。章氏致力於國粹之保存乃是他一生中最重要之使命。

第六章：「章氏與近代中國之文化保守主義」。此章將分析章氏之國粹概念與其他國粹派間之異同；並且欲對文化保守主義在近代中國思想史中之重要性及章氏在此一思潮中所扮演之角色加以評估。

第七章：「結論」。

CHAPTER 1

INTRODUCTION

Chang Ping-lin was born in Yü-hang, Chekiang, in 1869. Early in his life, he was educated by his family, especially by his maternal grandfather, who taught him Chinese classics and history, and told him stories of Ming loyalists resisting the Manchus as well. In 1890, Chang continued his studies at the Ku-ching Academy, where he studied philology and classics under Yü Yüeh, a prominent Han Learning scholar of the Late Ch'ing.

While Chang was still studying at the academy, he became involved in politics in 1895. He joined K'ang Yu-wei's Ch'iang-hsüeh hui in 1895, and the editorial staff of the reform journal, the Shih-wu pao in 1896. In this way, Chang started his new career as a political activist.

After the failure of the 1898 Reform Movement, Chang did not become openly a revolutionary until 1900, when he realized that the Manchu government was unable to defend the nation in the Boxer Uprising. In 1903, the Su-pao carried Chang's radical articles, in which he openly attacked the Manchus and even denounced the Kuang-hsü Emperor as a "little clown". Eventually, it brought forth the Su-pao case. The Manchu government ordered the suppression of the Su-pao and the arrest of Chang Ping-lin. As a result, Chang was jailed for three years.

After Chang's release from prison in 1906, he was invited to join the T'ung-meng hui, and was made editor-in-chief of the Min-pao. In 1908, the Min-pao was closed down by the Japanese authorities at the request of the Manchu government. On October 10, 1911, the Wu-ch'ang Uprising succeeded, and within a few months a new republic was born.

After the founding of the republic, Chang served as advisor of Sun Yat-sen and Yüan Shih-k'ai respectively. Yüan also appointed him as the Frontier Defense Commissioner of the Three Eastern Provinces. During the Republican Era, Chang was also involved in many political activities. He was involved in the movement for the confederation of autonomous provinces in the 1920's in the anti-communist movement in 1925, and in the crusade against the Japanese invasion in the 1930's. Apart from his involvement in politics, Chang devoted most of his energies to teaching and to classical scholarship, and sought to preserve China's national essence.

The main thrust of this study is to explore the life and thought of Chang Ping-lin and in particular, his concern to preserve the national essence (kuo-ts'ui 國粹) of China and the association between this objective and his involvement in politics. Chang began to be involved in politics from 1895, and throughout the early 1930s he was active in the political arena. However, politics was perceived by Chang mainly as a means to fulfill the ultimate goal of the preservation of the national essence. The presentation will show many features of the crucial period of intellectual change in modern China, the years from the 1890s to the 1930s. Although this change owed a great deal to indigenous developments within China in the late nineteenth century, the primary force behind this change was the "Western impact."

The decade of the 1890s witnessed a drastic intellectual change provoked mainly by the half-century of Western expansion in China and its severe new forms.[1] Now foreign aggression entered a new stage.[2] In 1894 China was defeated in the Sino-Japanese War, a defeat which seemed particularly shocking to most Chinese because the victor was a small non-Western state most Chinese regarded as far inferior to China in both culture and power.[3] In the wake of China's humiliating defeat, Western powers -- France, Russia, Great Britain, and Germany -- successively wrenched important territorial and economic concessions from China. The day of China's dissolution seemed impending, and an atmosphere of national crisis was thus created.[4] Therefore, many Chinese intellectuals began to realize that unless China implemented fundamental reforms,

---

[1]Chang Hao, "Intellectual Change and the Reform Movement, 1890-8" in Denis Twitchett and John K. Fairbank, eds., The Cambridge History of China (Cambridge: Cambridge University Press, 1980), v. 11, p. 274.

[2]Ibid.

[3]Ibid., p. 291.

[4]See Samuel C. Chu, Reformer in Modern China: Chang Chien, 1853-1926 (New York: Columbia University Press, 1965), p. 5.

14

the survival of the nation was dubious. Under this intellectual ferment, K'ang Yu-wei's 康有爲 (1858-1927) reformism was the most prominent of the day.

In the summer of 1898 K'ang's Hundred Days Reform (Pai-jih wei-hsin 百日維新) occurred. Although K'ang and his followers failed in their attempt to reform China, the basic cause of their action, the desire to strengthen the nation remained. [5] In 1900, the Boxer Uprising occurred. The Boxers, a mystical patriotic group, embarked on a campaign to drive the foreigners out of China by force. The result of this event was China's ultimate humiliation at the hands of the allied forces of the eight powers.[6] This event proved that the Manchu government was incapable of defending the nation. Therefore, many intellectuals turned against the Manchu dynasty, and joined the camp of revolution. Forces of revolution were then making headway. In 1911 the revolutionary movement culminated in the termination of imperial rule. The founding of the republic saw China still in political chaos. After the death of Yüan Shih-K'ai 袁世凱 (1859-1916), the new republic was endangered by warlordism and intensified imperialism. In the midst of such chaos, Chinese intellectuals launched the New Culture

---

[5]Ibid., pp. 5-6.

[6]Ibid., p.6.

Movement (<u>Hsin-wen-hua yun-tung</u> 新文化運動) in 1917, the aim of which was to rejuvenate the nation.[7]

After 1900 when national crisis intensified, two distinct approaches were adopted by Chinese intellectuals in order to save China.[8] On the one hand, many intellectuals concerned themselves merely with the protection of the nation as a political entity rather with the preservation of the traditional culture. After the founding of the republic, some intellectuals such as the New Culturists even regarded the traditional culture as a barrier to China's innovation. Thus, they asserted that in order to regenerate China, the traditional culture should be rejected.[9] On the other, another group of intellectuals, who were well versed in Chinese classics and history, were concerned with both the survival of the nation and the preservation of China's cultural heritage.[10]

Chang was the leading intellectual within the latter group. Chang perceived the nation not only as a political entity but also as a cultural entity. Thus, while he

---

[7]See Chow Tse-tsung, <u>The May Fourth Movement: Intellectual Revolution in Modern China</u> (Cambridge: Harvard University Press, 1960), p. 41.

[8]Shen Sung-ch'iao 沈松僑 , <u>Hsüeh-heng-p'ai yü wu-ssu shih-ch'i te fan Hsin-wen-hua-yün-tung</u> 學衡派與五四時期的反新文化運動 (Taipei: National Taiwan University Press, 1984), p. 270.

[9]<u>Ibid</u>.

[10]<u>Ibid</u>., p. 274.

was concerned about the search for wealth and power of the nation, his ultimate concern was to preserve China's culture from extinction from external forces.

Chang had first become a reformer in 1895, then a prominent revolutionist. After the founding of the republic, Chang served as privy counselor of Sun Yat-sen 孫逸仙 (1866-1925), president of the provisional government in Nanking. After Yuan Shih-k'ai was elected as provisional president in Peking, Chang also served as his senior adviser, before Yuan appointed Chang as the Frontier Defense Commissioner of the Three Eastern Provinces (Tung-san-sheng ch'ou-pien-shih 東三省籌邊使). During the Republican Era, Chang was also involved in many political activities. Apart from his involvement in politics, Chang devoted most of his energies to teaching and to classical scholarship, and sought to preserve Chinese traditional culture. As a leading scholar of the time, Chang was also involved in the National Essence Movement (Kuo-ts'ui yün-tung 國粹運動) in the early Republican Era. He played an important role in both the political arena and the intellectual world.

I have chosen this topic partly because Chang's political and intellectual activities span the critical forty years of phenomenal change in China. Chang had reached his mental adulthood in the 1890s and by the 1930s was active at the center of China's political arena and intellectual world. However, despite his importance as one of the major Chinese thinkers, scholars and political activists of this century, Chang has received little attention in the West. One reason for this neglect is that Chang wrote in a dense classical style -- to be precise, the so-called

Wei-Chin (220-420 A.D.) style, and his thought had numerous Western and

indigenous intellectual influences, all of which make his writings exceedingly difficult

to understand. Another reason is that Chang does not fit neatly into the

categories, conservative or radical, which are used by modern historians as an

explanatory device in probing intellectual life in modern China. The

conservative/radical classification, though useful as an explanatory category, is not

suitable for thinkers like Chang Ping-lin, for Chang, though he can be described

as a conservative, or more precisely a cultural conservative, was also a political

radical.

Even the scant scholarly treatment Chang has received in the West[11] fails

---

[11]There are only few articles in English: Charlotte Furth, "The Sage as Rebel: The Inner World of Chang Ping-lin" in Charlotte Furth, ed., The Limits of Change: Essays on Conservative Alternatives in Republican China (Cambridge: Harvard University Press, 1976), pp. 113-150; Joshua A Fogel, "Race and Class in Chinese Historiography: Divergent Interpretations of Zhang Bing-lin and Anti-Manchuism in the 1911 Revolution", Modern China, 3:3 (July, 1977), pp. 346-375. Warren Sun, "Chang Ping-lin and His Political Thought" Paper on Far Eastern History (September, 1985), pp. 57-69; One chapter on Chang Ping-lin in both Michael Gasster's Chinese Intellectuals and the Revolution of 1911: The Birth of Modern Chinese Radicalism (Seattle: University of Washington Press, 1968), pp. 190-227, and Chang Hao's Chinese Intelletuals in Crisis: Search for Order and Meaning (1890-1911) (Berkeley: University of California Press, 1987), pp. 104-145; and a biography of Chang in BDRC, v. 1, pp. 92-98. In 1989 Young-tsu Wong published a book on Chang: Search for Modern Nationalism: Zhang Binglin and Revolutionary China, 1869-1936 (Oxford: Oxford University Press). In this book, he focused his study mainly on Chang's political ideas and activities and made great effort to evaluate Chang's contribution to revolution and politics. However, he failed to probe Chang's core idea, the preservation of the national essence and its significance to Chang's political ideas. Chinese scholars have also published

18

to assess adequately his life and thought. His ideas, when taken together, are considered to be contradictory. During his life, he was at different times a supporter of reform and at other times of revolution. His career was marked by ironies. As a political revolutionary, he called for the preservation of China's national essence. After the founding of the republic, this prominent revolutionary switched from support of Sun Yat-sen to Yüan Shih-k'ai, and later denounced Yüan. He was known as a great classical scholar, but he criticized Confucianism. Furthermore, he advocated republicanism and yet condemned representative government as a remnant of feudalism. Much of this appearance of inconsistency, however, is reduced, or even eliminated, if we keep in mind his efforts to preserve the national essence, which is the most consistent thread in this thinking, for all of his differing positions were assumed only as a means to serve an ultimate goal: the preservation of the national essence. This concern was always the unifier of apparent opposites.

The preservation of the national essence was the core idea and the most fundamental and constant characteristic of his thinking, and the foundation for his political action. A thorough study on Chang's life and thought is necessary to show

---

on Chang, for example, see Li Zehou, "Zhang Taiyan As a Revolutionary and a Thinker" in The 1911 Revolution: A Retrospective after 70 years (Peking: New World Press; 1983), pp. 183-202; Mabel Lee, "Chang Ping-lin's Concept of Self and Society: Questions of Constancy and Continuity after the 1911 Revolution" in Conference on the Early History of China, 1917-1927 (Taipei: Chung-yang yen-chiu-yüan chin-tai-shih yen-chiu-so, 1984), v. 2, pp. 593-628.

this dimension of his thought. Unfortunately, both Chinese and Western scholars have overlooked this core idea,[12] and thus have limited our understanding of Chang's thought. Therefore, there is a strong need for a reassessment of Chang Ping-lin. It is also hoped that my study of Chang Ping-lin will begin this effort and provide a better understanding of his life and thought.

My study of Chang Ping-lin began with an exhaustive exploration of the primary and secondary source data in Chinese and English. Through these sources I have tried to show the life and thought of Chang Ping-lin in late imperial and early Republican China as a means to explore more fully intellectual change in general in this period. This is not an intellectual biography of Chang per se, but my approach is that of intellectual history. Chang's thought reflects an important dimension of that change, for it illustrates the tension between political and cultural ideals among the elite of his generation. Moreover, his lifelong commitment to the preservation of the national essence foreshadows and important trend in the 1910s - 1930s, the so-called National Essence Movement. This cultural conservatism constituted an important element in efforts to counter wholesale westernization in early republican times. The New Culture Movement was in part a response to such cultural conservatism. With the rise of radical anti-traditionalism and skeptism among the New Culturists towards their tradition, due to his concern for the preservation of the national essence, Chang assumed his responsibility to defend

---

[12]There are several studies on Chang in Chinese.

traditional culture. He was also involved in the National Essence Movement.

Thus, analyzing the life and works of Chang Ping-lin will, I believe, contribute to a better understanding of the life and thought of Chang, of the relationship between political radicalism and cultural conservatism in that era, and of the role played by cultural conservatism generally in modern Chinese history. My study will begin with the examination of Chang's early life and intellectual background, which provides the basis as an understanding for the formation of Chang's core idea. Since the preservation of the national essence is Chang's core idea and the foundation for his political actions, the following chapter is devoted to manifest Chang's effort to preserve the national essence, and to analyze the origins of his concept of the national essence, as well as its scope and meaning.

Chang became politically engaged from 1895, and throughout the early 1930s he played an important role in the political arena. However, for Chang, politics did not mean an all-embracing activity[13], but was mainly as a means to fulfill the goal of the preservation of China's cultural heritage. I will discuss Chang's political activities and their association with his main concern in two chapters.

Chang's commitment to the preservation of the national essence paved the way for the National Essence Movement, a culturally conservative movement. Chang's thought also illustrated the tension between political and cultural ideals,

---

[13]See Warren Sun, op. cit., p. 57.

particularly among the national essence intellectuals. Thus, one whole chapter will be allocated for the examination of the significance of cultural conservatism in modern China, and for showing Chang's contributions to this intellectual current, and his place in Chinese cultural conservatism.

CHAPTER 2

CHANG PING-LIN'S EARLY LIFE
AND INTELLECTUAL BACKGROUND

Chang Ping-lin 章炳麟 was born into a scholar-gentry family in Yü-hang 餘杭 , Chekiang 浙江 , on January 12, 1869.[1] The general area where he was born and raised is situated within the Kiangnan 江南 region (the area south of the lower reaches of the Yangtze River 長江),[2] a heartland of commerce, communication and culture. The emerging prosperity of Kiangnan in late imperial China had been preceded in earlier centuries by a large-scale migration of population from north China to the south. This massive influx of migrants from the north resulted in a high population density in the fertile Kiangnan region and stimulated urbanization and commercialization. As the economy of

---

[1]Chang Ping-lin's ancestors moved to Yü-hang about five hundred years before his birth. See TTNP, p. 1. Chang Ping-lin's original name was Hsüeh-ch'eng 學乘 , his courtesy name (tzu 字) was Mei-shu 枚叔 , and his literary name (hao 號) was T'ai-yen 太炎. The number of names or pen names that Chang used at one time or another is about twenty. See NPCP, v. 1, p. 2. Also see BDRC, v. 1, p. 92.

[2]During the Ch'ing dynasty, Kiangnan, the region between Shanghai and Nanking, was generally referred to as parts of Kiangsu, Anhwei and the whole territory of Chekiang. See Benjamin Elman, "The Unravelling of Neo-Confucianism: the Lower Yangtze Academic Community in Late Imperial China" (Ph.D. Dissertation, University of Pennsylvania, 1980), p. 14, 7n., and Yoshinobu Shiba, "Urbanization and the Development of Markets in the Lower Yangtze Valley", in John Winthrop Haeger, ed., Crisis and Prosperity in Sung China (Tucson: The University of Arizona Press, 1975), p. 15.

Kiangnan became more commercialized and more prosperous, merchants from other areas came to Kiangnan for commerce and trade. As a result, the mercantile sector of the economy grew rapidly and Kiangnan became the most economically advanced region of the country. During the Ch'ing dynasty, with the growth of wealth and an increase of leisure time, merchants showed a strong interest in the support of scholarship, which in turn contributed to the development of k'ao-cheng 考 證 scholarship.[3] Being the richest and most cultured region of the country, Kiangnan had long been renowned for its strong support of scholarship and production of large numbers of scholars. In the latter half of the nineteenth century, Kiangnan became a center of reformist and revolutionary political activities, with student groups and scholars constituting a mainstream of this movement.[4]

Chang Ping-lin's great-grandfather, Chang Chün 章均 (1769-1832), was named an "added student" of state schools at the district level (hsien-hsüeh tseng-

---

[3]Elman, op. cit., pp.11-20, and Shiba, op. cit., pp. 13-48. See also E. A. Kracke, Jr., "Sung Society: Change within Tradition", Far Eastern Quarterly, v. 14 (1954-55) pp. 479-488 and Tu Wei-yün 杜維運 , Hsüeh-shu yü shih-pien 學術與世變 (Taipei: Huan-yü ch'u-pan she, 1971), p. 118.

[4]See Mary Backus Rankin, Early Chinese Revolutionaries: Radical Intellectuals in Shanghai and Chekiang, 1902-1911 (Cambridge: Harvard University Press, 1971), p. 3.

kuang-sheng 縣學增廣生   );[5] he subsequently served as an Assistant

Instructor (hsün-tao 訓導) in a Confucian school in Hai-yen 海鹽 district,

Chekiang province.[6] Apart from his teaching, Chang Chün is also said to have

been a generous man and good at managing finances. At the age of eighteen, he

received and carried on the family business founded by his ancestors. After

several years of his personal management, Chang Chün became very rich. In

1828, he founded the T'iao-nan 苕南 Academy in Yü-hang district, which was later

destroyed by fire about 1860.[7] Chang Chün also established a charitable estate

(i-chuang 義莊),[8] which provided regular relief and aid to poor clan members

---

[5]"Added student" is a designation for students admitted to state schools at the prefectural (chou 州 , fu 府) and lower levels of the administration. In the Ch'ing period, the status of the added student was higher than that of the supplementary student (fu-hsüeh-sheng 府學生 , fu-sheng 府生) and below that of the stipend student (lin-sheng 稟生).See Charles O. Hucker, ed., A Dictionary of Official Titles in Imperial China (Stanford: Stanford University Press, 1985), p. 522.

[6]This account of Chang Ping-lin's ancestors is based on the following sources: Ch'u Ch'eng-po 褚成博 ed., Kuang-hsü Yü-hang hsien-chih kao 光緒餘杭 縣志稿 (Draft Gazetteer of Yü-hang County in the Kuang-hsü Era), v. 4. This gazetteer contains brief biographies of a number of Chang's ancestors; and CTYCC, v. 5, pp. 194-196, which contains a brief outline of his predecessors by Chang himself. The BDRC is incorrect in saying that "there is a singular lack of information about his ancestry and his parents," v. 1, p. 92.

[7]See also Ch'u, op. cit., v. 1.

[8]The system of charitable estates or charitable lands was originated with the Northern Sung (960-1127) statesman Fan Chung-yen 范仲淹 (989-1052), who, in the middle of the eleventh century, set up this system to aid poor clan members. See Hui-chen Wang Liu, "An Analysis of Chinese Clan Rules: Confucian Theories in Action", pp. 63-96; Denis Twitchett, "The Fan Clan's Charitable Estate, 1050-1760", pp. 97-133. Both are in David S. Nivison and Arthur F. Wright, eds.,

and helped pay their expenses for such things as weddings and funerals. He also founded a charitable school (i-shu 義塾   or i-hsüeh 義學   ) to educate the young men of the clan.

Chang Ping-lin's grandfather, Chang Chien 章鑒 (1802-1863), was named a "supplementary student" at the district school (hsien-hsüeh fu-hsüeh-sheng 縣學府學生   ). However, Chang Chien elected not to pursue a civil service career.   In his day, the family was still quite wealthy, and he did not feel economically pressed to seek public office. Later, because of his own scholarly interests, he acquired an impressive personal library of nearly 5,000 volumes (chüan 卷) of Sung, Yüan, and Ming dynasty editions. However, except for the catalogue of this collection, almost everything was lost in the early 1860s when Taiping rebels overran the area. Nevertheless, the prior existence of this collection exerted some influence on Chang Ping-lin in his early years. In his teens, Chang Ping-lin was educated by his father, who, while tutoring him in the Chinese classics and history, frequently showed him the catalogue of this collection. In his middle years, Chang Chien took up the study of traditional Chinese medicine (i-shu 醫 術). From then on, he remained in his hometown, Yü-hang, practicing medicine and serving the poor when they were sick. Because of his own personal wealth, Chang Chien never accepted payment from his patients.

Confucianism in Action (Stanford: Stanford University Press), 1959.

Chang Ping-lin's father, Chang Chün 章濬 (1825-1890), was a "stipend student" in government schools at the district level (hsien-hsüeh lin-sheng 縣學 稟生). From his early childhood, Chang Chün was fond of study. The family library was a valuable aid in those endeavors. As an adult, he was skilled in poetry and a published writer.[9] Chang Chün was also skilled in traditional medicine. And still later, like his grandfather and father, Chang Ping-lin also manifested an interest in the study and practice of medicine.[10]

In 1861, when Chang Chün was thirty-six years of age, his family had to flee Taiping armies. After that rebellion was suppressed, the fortunes of the Chang family were in disarray. During the conflict the Hsiang army had appropriated part of their charitable lands when they were absent from the scene. However, after considerable effort, Chang Chün was able to recover most of their property. And once again he and his family found themselves in comfortable circumstances.

Chang Chün had once been on the list of Expectant Appointees as District Magistrates (hou-hsüan chih-hsien 候選知縣). In 1867, the prefect of Hangchow (Hang-chou) 杭州 invited Chang Chün to join his secretarial staff (mu-yu 幕友 or mu-fu 幕府), and he accepted. Shortly after the birth of his son

---

[9]Chang Chün wrote a book entitled Ch'un-feng ts'ao-lu sheng-kao 春風 草廬賸稿 (A Surplus Draft Written in Ch'un-feng Humble Cottage). See Ch'u, op. cit., v. 3. Ch'un-feng ts'ao-lu 春風草廬 was the name for Chang Chien's study.

[10]See NPCP, v. 1, pp. 3-4. For a list of Chang Ping-lin's writings on medicine, see T'ai-yen hsien-sheng chu-shu mu-lu 太炎先生著述目錄 (Mr. [Chang] T'ai-yen's Catalogue of Writings), in TTNP, pp. 69-142.

Ping-lin in 1869, he resigned that post and returned to his hometown, Yü-hang, where he served as an Assistant Instructor at a district school.[11]

As members of the middle gentry class, Chang Ping-lin's ancestors were well grounded in classical studies, and he was also to receive a similar education.[12] In acquiring the rudiments of classical scholarship, Chang was guided by members of his own family, especially by his maternal grandfather, Chu Tso-ch'ing 朱左卿 (b. 1815), who taught him the Confucian classics and history.[13] At the age of nine, while still quite young, his grandfather introduced him to the basic principles of philological analysis as that methodology applied to the ancient classics.[14] After four years under the tutelage of his maternal grandfather, Chang tells us that he began to acquire an understanding of the Confucian texts.[15] In 1880, when his maternal grandfather returned to his ancestral home in Hai-yen, Chekiang, the supervision of his studies devolved upon his father and his eldest brother, Chang Chien 章籛 (1853-1928), who revealed

---

[11]See Chiang I-hua姜義華, Chang T'ai-yen ssu-hsiang yen-chiu 章太炎思想 研究 . (Shanghai: Jen-min ch'u-pan she, 1985), p. 3. For details of mu-fu, see Kenneth E. Folsom, Friends, Guests, and Colleagues: the Mu-fu System in the Late Ch'ing Period (Berkeley: University of California Press, 1968).

[12]TTNP, pp. 2-3. Also see BDRC, v. 1, p. 92.

[13]TTNP, p.2.

[14]Ibid.

[15]Ibid. Chang himself did not mention the texts he read at that time.

to him key aspects of classical learning.[16] In his teens, he began to read the Shih-san-ching chu-shu 十三經注疏 (Commentaries and Annotations on the Thirteen Classics), the Hsüeh-hai t'ang ching-chieh 學海堂經解 (Hsüeh-hai Hall's Exegesis of the Classics),[17] and individual works by noted Han Learning scholars of the Ch'ing dynasty.[18] From then on, he became a devoted student of the classics.

Although Chang Ping-lin developed an avid interest in classical scholarship during his youth, he did not take the civil service examinations.[19] The reason for this was apparently a repugnance for the Manchu rulers of the Ch'ing dynasty.[20]

---

[16]Ibid, pp. 2-3.

[17]The Hsüeh-hai t'ang ching-chieh was better known under the title Huang-Ch'ing ching-chieh 皇清經解 (The Imperial Ch'ing Exergesis of the Classics). This scholarly collection was published by the Hsüeh-hai t'ang in Canton in 1829, and contained 188 different works by 74 authors in 1408 chuan. It was devoted exclusively to evidential scholarship. See Chiang, op. cit., pp. 11-12; Benjamin Elman, From Philosophy to Philology (Cambridge: Harvard University Press, 1984), p. 90.

[18]The texts he read at this time were: Yin-hsüeh wu-shu 章學五書 (Five Books on Phonology) by Ku Yen-wu 顧炎武 (1613-1682); Ching-i shu-wen 經義述聞 (Interpretations of the Classics Heard from [My Father]) by Wang Yin-chih 王引之 (1766-1834); and Erh-ya i-shu 爾雅義疏 (Commentary on the Meaning of the Erh-ya) by Hao I-hsing 郝懿行 (1757-1825). See NPCP, v. 1, p. 9.

[19]Ibid., v. 1, p. 7.

[20]Ibid., v. 1, p. 10; See also Feng Tzu-yu 馮自由 , Chung-hua min-kuo k'ai-kuo ch'ien ke-ming shih 中華民國開國前革命史 (Shanghai: Ko-ming shih pien-chi she, 1928), v. 1, p. 111.

Chang's anti-Manchu sentiments were inspired during his childhood. At about the age of twelve, apart from his study of the classics, his maternal grandfather told him stories of late Ming loyalists who resisted the Manchu invasion. In this way, Chang began to acquire a strong sense of ethnic identity on the one hand and a hatred for the Manchus on the other.[21] These sentiments were further aroused by his reading of the Tung-hua lu 東華錄 (Notes from the Manchu Archives) and the Ming-chi pai-shih 明季稗史 (Unofficial Historical Writings of the End of the Ming Era), which described the numerous persecutions of Han Chinese by the Manchus.[22]

Chang's own reminiscences also suggest that his aversion to the existing regime had something to do with his family precepts (chia-hsün 家訓). According to his own account, his father once told him that inasmuch as his family had maintained an enmity for the Manchus since the early days of the conquest, it had become the custom for his family members to be buried in Chinese ceremonial dress instead of Manchu dress.[23] It was from family precepts of this kind that

---

[21]NPCP, v. 1, pp. 5-6.

[22]Ibid., v. 1, p. 6.

[23]After the Manchu conquest of China, the Chinese people were required to adopt Manchu customs as a symbol of submission. This included shaving the front of the head and growing a queue, and the adoption of the Manchu dress. Those who disobeyed these injunctions were severely punished. See Huang Hung-shou 黃鴻壽 , Ch'ing-shih chi-shih pen-mo 清史紀事本末 (Taipei: San-min shu-chü, 1959), v. 5: 27, 29; Ta-Ch'ing li-ch'ao shih-lu 大清歷朝實錄 (Taipei: Hua-lien ch'u-pan she, 1964), Shun-chih reign, v. 5: 52; Wang Hsien-

Chang also derived his anti-Manchu convictions.[24] Although he developed these sentiments early in life, they did not immediately turn him against the existing regime. Nevertheless, the fact that he was unwilling to sit for the civil service examinations, the main avenue to position and wealth at that time, may be interpreted as a distaste for the Manchus, although it is also true that many scholars of the later imperial times chose the life of scholarship and seclusion over careers in public service. Thereafter, he concentrated his efforts on the study of Chinese history and the classics in preparation for a life of scholarship.[25]

In 1890, after his father's death, Chang went to Hang-chou and entered the Ku-ching ching-she 詁經精舍 Academy (Refined Study for the Explication of the Classics),[26] a citadel of Confucian learning. There evidential scholarship as practiced by the School of Han Learning was in vogue, and he studied

_____

ch'ien 王先謙 , ed., Shih-i ch'ao Tung-hua lu 十一朝東華錄 (Shanghai: T'u-shu chi-ch'eng chen-pen chü, 1887), Shun-chih reign, v. 4: 12-13; v. 5: 1-2; v. 20: 8. However, it was also true that Chinese were allowed to be buried in Ming clothes.

[24]NPCP, v. 1, p. 10.

[25]Ibid.

[26]This academy was founded in 1801 by the famous scholar-official Juan Yüan 阮元 (1764-1849), when he was serving as governor of Chekiang, and destroyed during the Taiping Rebellion (1850-1864). See ECCP, v. 1, p. 400; Elman, From Philosophy to Philology, pp. 109, 250; For a detailed account of this academy, See Chang Yin 張崟 , "Ku-ching ching-she ch'u-kao 詁經精舍初稿 ". Wen-lan hsüeh-pao 文瀾學報 2:1 (March, 1936) pp. 1-47.

philology, history and the classics under Yü Yüeh　俞樾　(1821-1907),[27] a friend

of his father and a scholar of great renown.[28]　Yü Yüeh's teachings basically

followed the tradition of Ch'ien-Chia　乾嘉　(Ch'ien-lung　乾隆　and Chia-

ch'ing　嘉慶　reign periods, 1736-1840) Han Learning, which represented an

accommodation of both the Ancient Text (ku-wen　古文) and New Text (chin-wen

今文) persuasions.[29] The distinction between the Ancient and New Text schools

had its origin in the Ch'in dynasty (221-206 B.C.) burning of the books in 213 B.C.,

when the First Emperor of Ch'in (Ch'in Shih-huang-ti　秦始皇帝　) attempted to

destroy most of the ancient classics.[30]

---

[27]ECCP, v. 2, pp. 944-945.

[28]Chang Ping-lin's father had been serving as supervisor (chien-yüan　監院) of the Ku-ching ching-she Academy, a position which was only secondary to the director (yüan-chang　院長), and was also appointed by the provincial governor (hsün-fu　巡撫), while Yü Yüeh was the director of the academy. See Chiang, op. cit., pp. 8, 11-14.

[29]Han Learning scholars in the mid-Ch'ing period modelled themselves on the master Cheng Hsüan 鄭玄(127-200), who had combined the New and Ancient Text persuasions in his annotations of the classics. See Ibid., p. 23; Wang Fan-sen 王汎森 , Chang T'ai-yen te ssu-hsiang　章太炎的思想 , 1868-1919 (Taipei: Shih-pao ch'u-pan she, 1985), p. 24.

[30]The following account of the dispute between the New and Ancient Text schools is primarily based on Chou Yü-t'ung 周予同 , Ching chin-ku-wen hsüeh 經今古文學　(Taipei: Commercial Press, 1967). Also see Lu Yüan-chün 盧元駿 , "Ching-hsüeh chi fa-chan yü chin-ku-wen chih fen-ho" 經學之發展與今古文之分合 in Wang Ching-chih　王靜芝 , et al., Ching-hsüeh yen-chiu lun-chi 經學研究論集(Taipei: Li-ming ch'u-pan she, 1981), pp.81-102; Wang Ching-chih, Ching-hsüeh t'ung-lun　經學通論　(Taipei: Kuo-li pien-i kuan, 1972), v. 1, pp. 79-86; Liang Ch'i-ch'ao, Intellectual Trends in the Ch'ing Period, tr. Immanuel C. Y. Hsü (Cambridge: Harvard University Press, 1959), pp. 85-87.

With the rise of the Former Han dynasty (206 B.C. - 8 A.D.), copies of the ancient books ordered destroyed by the Ch'in were found still to exist, while other editions were recovered from the memories of scholars. All these texts were written in the current script (chin-wen今文) or in characters of clerical style (li-shu 隸書), which had come into general use in Ch'in-Han times. These editions of the ancient texts were accepted as authentic by scholars and by the state. Thus, the New Text School, which based itself on these texts, dominated the intellectual world of the Former Han period. However, toward the end of the reign of Emperor Wu 武 (r. 140-87 B.C.) of the Former Han, Prince Kung of Lu (Lu Kung-wang 魯恭王) claimed to have found, in the wall of Confucius' home, older versions of some of the classical texts. These were the versions adopted by the so-called Ancient Text School. This school took its name from versions of the classics written in an archaic script of the Chou dynasty (1111-249 B.C.). While many scholars of the time suspected that these ancient texts were indeed authentic, controversy between the New and Ancient Text schools did not arise until the end of the Former Han period, when Liu Hsin 劉歆 (46 B.C. - 23 A.D.) attempted to establish the ancient texts as the basis of learning in state schools during the reign of Emperor Ai 哀 (r. 6 - 1 B.C.). Although this attempt was not successful, it did give rise to a dispute between these two schools of learning.

The difference between these two schools was at first textual in nature. However, the controversy was not limited to textual matters alone, for it involved fundamental ideological differences as well. Generally speaking, in Han times the members of the New Text School tended to favor the use of the yin-yang 陰陽 and "Five Elements" (wu-hsing 五行) cosmological concepts to interpret Confucian doctrines. They also showed a strong inclination to use apocryphal texts (ch'an-wei 讖緯) in the interpretation of the classics. In this way, they attempted to elevate Confucius to the position of a sort of Messiah, or "uncrowned king" (su-wang 素王), who, they thought, had created the Six Classics (liu-ching 六經), and that great principles lay behind his subtle words (wei-yen ta-i 微言大 義). The Ancient Text scholars, on the other hand, regarded Confucius as a great teacher and a transmitter or preserver of the ancient culture, instead of a creator of the classics. They maintained that the classics were purely historical documents and rejected what they regarded as the "superstitious interpretation" of the classics by the New Text School.[31] While these textual and ideological differences existed, there were still other causes for this dispute. This had to do with a

---

[31]See Chan Wing-tsit, A Source Book in Chinese Philosophy (Princeton: Princeton University Press, 1969), pp. 314-315, 723; Chen Chi-yun, Hsün Yüeh (A.D. 148-209): The Life and Reflections of an Early Medieval Confucian (New York: Cambridge University Press, 1975), pp. 15-17; Fung Yu-lan, A History of Chinese Philosophy, tr. Derk Bodde (Princeton: Princeton University Press, 1953), v. 2, pp. 7-8, 133-136; Wm. Theodore de Bary et al., Sources of Chinese Tradition (New York: Columbia University Press, 1961), pp. 261-262. For a detailed discussion of the differences between these two schools, see Tjan Tjoe Som, Po-hu-t'ung (Leiden: E.J. Brill, 1949), v. 1, pp. 137-145.

struggle between the two camps for positions of favor and influence in government, and the wealth and power that entailed.[32]

In 136 B.C., Emperor Wu ordered the establishment of appointive positions for Erudites of the Five Classics (wu-ching po-shih　五經博士　). Students on government stipends were assigned to study under the guidance of these Erudites at the Imperial Academy (t'ai-hsüeh　太學　) in preparation for their selection to governmental offices. The number of official students, the so-called po-shih ti-tzu 博士弟子　(pupils of the Erudites), gradually increased with the passage of time. By the end of the Former Han Dynasty, their number had increased from 50 to 3,000. In Later Han times, the number of official students at the Imperial Academy exceeded 30,000. Almost all of these Erudites were specialists in the New Text versions of the classics. Since official recognition of one or the other school meant imperial favor and political influence, this naturally induced rivalry among scholars seeking appointments as Erudites, for not only were Erudites employed as governmental officials, they were also teachers of future officials, the po-shih ti-tzu. Thus, when Liu Hsin endeavored to gain official recognition for the Ancient Texts, he was severly attacked by the current Erudites, for they and their disciples were chiefly concerned about the maintenance of their positions.

---

[32]Ch'ien Mu 錢穆 , Kuo-hsüeh kai-lun　國學概論 (Taipei: Commercial Press, 1974), p. 81.

From that moment on, the debate between the two schools continued,[33] and with the restoration of the Han, the Later Han Dynasty (25-220), the Ancient Text School flourished, but it never received official recognition during Later Han times. It was much in vogue, however, for those scholars who were not members of the imperial bureaucracy.[34]

Toward the end of the Later Han era, several great Ancient Text scholars, such as Fu Ch'ien 服虔 (2nd century A.D.) and Ma Yung (or Jung) 馬融 (76-166) appeared, and the Ancient Text School gained ascendancy in the scholarly community. One of Ma Yung's disciples, Cheng Hsüan, came in time to dominate the intellectual world, and he attempted to eliminate the main distinctions in exegetical scholarship between the New and Ancient Text Schools. His extensive commentaries on the New and Ancient Text versions of the classics served largely to end the dispute between the two schools until mid-Ch'ing times.

During the mid-Ch'ing, the practice of evidential research (k'ao-cheng, lit., "search for evidence" and meaning the close analytical study of the classical texts employing inductive and comparative methods) reached a new level of maturity and eventually dominated the intellectual world of the time. Although k'ao-cheng scholarship reached its zenith during the Ch'ien-Chia era, its roots could be traced back to the seventeenth century, or indeed to Northern Sung times (960-1126) or

---

[33]See Tjan Tjoe Som, op. cit., v. 1, pp. 84, 88.

[34]Ibid., v. 1, p. 151; and Fung, op. cit., p. 135.

even to T'ang (618-907). In early T'ang times, K'ung Ying-ta 孔穎達 (574-648)

had edited the <u>Standard Commentaries on the Five Classics</u> (<u>Wu-ching cheng-i</u>

五經正義),[35] which was later established as the standard reference

for the civil service examinations.[36] However, a new trend in the textual criticism

emerged to challenge the authority of K'ung's orthodox commentaries. Scholars

associated with this movement advocated a return to the classics themselves as

a basis for understanding the true meaning of the sages. Although these scholars

dared to call tradition into question, they did not go far enough in questioning that

tradition. However, most importantly they did attempt to get at the truth by

emphasizing the classics and relying less on the commentaries.[37]

---

[35]Actually, the <u>Wu-ching cheng-i</u> was not edited by K'ung alone, but by him and other T'ang scholars. It is said that originally there were Six Classics, one of which, the <u>Book of Music</u> (<u>Yüeh-ching</u> 樂經) was lost before the third century B.C. The so-called Five Classics were the <u>Book of Songs</u> (<u>Shih-ching</u> 詩經), the <u>Book of History</u> (<u>Shu-ching</u> 書經), the <u>Book of Changes</u> (<u>I-ching</u> 易經), the <u>Book of Ceremony and Ritual</u> (<u>Li-ching</u> 禮經 or <u>I-li</u> 儀禮) and the <u>Spring and Autumn Annals</u> (<u>Ch'un-ch'iu</u> 春秋). However, in K'ung's <u>Wu-ching cheng-i</u>, the <u>Book of Ceremony and Ritual</u> was replaced by the <u>Book of Rites</u> (<u>Li-chi</u> 禮記).

[36]K'ung's orthodox commentaries was used as the standard text for the <u>ming-ching k'o</u> 明經科 (Classicist Category), one of several categories in the regular civil service examination system. In T'ang, the <u>ming-ching</u> examinations were highly popular and among the regular examinations second only to the <u>chin-shih</u> 進士 (presented scholars, that is, highest examination graduates) examinations in prestige. See Hucker, <u>op</u>. <u>cit</u>., p. 333.

[37]Edwin Pulleyblank, "Neo-Confucianism and Neo-Legalism in T'ang Intellectual Life, 755-805" in Arthur Wright, ed., <u>The Confucian Persuasion</u> (Stanford: Stanford University Press, 1960), pp. 77-114. See also Elman, <u>From Philosophy to Philology</u>, pp. 40-41 and Ma Tsung-huo 馬宗霍 , <u>Chung-kuo ching-hsüeh shih</u> 中國經學史 (Taipei: Commercial Press, 1979), pp. 180-200.

Although philology was not the major concern of Sung (960-1279) scholars, their labors in this field did result in important gains.[38] Following their T'ang predecessors, Sung scholars, after the Ch'ing-li era 慶曆 (1042-1048) of Jen-tsung 仁宗 (r. 1023-1063), began to discard K'ung's officially accepted interpretations of the Five Classics. They preferred instead to go back to the classics themselves and seek their own interpretations. In this spirit, Sun Fu 孫復 (992-1057) studied the Spring and Autumn Annals instead of its three commentaries.[39] In his study of the Annals, Sun "sought to express its essential meaning in the simplest terms, without regard to the diverse and confusing commentaries on the work."[40] Wang An-shih 王安石 studied the three classics and added his own commentaries,[41] which became the standard references for civil service examination candidates in Later Northern Sung times. Wang, in his commentaries on the classics, emphasized their general meaning instead of literal

---

[38]See Winston W. Lo, "Philology, an Aspect of Sung Rationalism", Chinese Culture 17:4 (Dec., 1976), pp. 1-26.

[39]P'i Hsi-jui 皮錫瑞 , Ching-hsüeh li-shih 經學歷史 (Taipei: I-wen yin-shu kuan, 1966), p. 202. See also Chan Wing-tsit, "Chu Hsi's Completion of Neo-Confucianism" in Wing-tsit Chan, Chu Hsi: Life and Thought (Hong Kong: The Chinese University Press, 1987), p. 130.

[40]See quote in de Bary, "A Reappraisal of Neo-Confucianism" in Arthur Wright, ed., Studies in Chinese Thought (Chicago: University of Chicago Press, 1953), p. 92.

[41]These three classics are the Book of Songs, the Book of History, and the Rituals of Chou. See Chan, "Chu hsi's Completion of Neo-Confucianism", p. 132.

38

interpretations.[42] With the rise of Neo-Confucianism in the eleventh century, Sung

Neo-Confucians went even further in their studies of the classics. They favored a

philosophical (i-li 義理) approach to the classics, which stressed the

apprehension of moral principles instead of literal meaning. They added their own

commentaries emphazing philosophical concepts sometimes going far afield of the

literal meaning of the texts.[43]

Parallel with this development was the growth of skepticism concerning the

authenticity of the classics in the eleventh century, especially during the years

1025-1100. Among Sung scholars, Ou-yang Hsiu 歐陽修 (1007-1072) raised

serious doubts about the classics. He questioned the authenticity of the Rituals

of Chou (Chou-li 周禮), of portions of the Book of Changes, and of the

prefaces to the Book of Songs (Shih-hsü 詩序). Su Shih 蘇軾 (1036-

1101) raised questions concerning both the Rituals of Chou and the Book of

History. Both Ssu-ma Kuang 司馬光 (1019-1101) and Li Kou 李覯

(1009-1059) were skeptical of the reliability of the Mencius (Meng-tzu 孟子). Chu

Hsi 朱熹 (1130-1200) even cast doubts upon many other books besides the

classics. And the spirit of this kind of skepticism toward the classics was carried

on by scholars during the Yüan (1271-1368) and Ming (1368-1644) periods. For

instance, Wu Ch'eng 吳澄 (1247-1331) of the Yüan and Mei Tsu 梅鷟 (fl. ca.

---

[42]de Bary, "A Reappraisal of Neo-Confucianism", p. 102.

[43]Chan, "Chu Hsi's Completion of Neo-Confucianism", p. 132.

1513) of the Ming, among others, concluded that the Ancient Text chapters of the Book of History were forgeries.[44]

Although the intellectual world of the Ming was dominated by Neo-Confucianism, especially by the Wang Yang-ming 王陽明 1472-1529) School, it was not entirely monopolized by the school. At least, since mid-Ming, scholars such as Yang Shen 楊愼 (1488-1559), Ch'en Ti 陳第 (1541-1617), and Chiao Hung 焦竑 (1541-1620), and others reoriented classical scholarship from philosophical interpretation to philological analysis. Yang Shen, a famous philologist attempted to reconstruct the ancient pronunciation of Chinese by the study of ancient rhyme schemes. Ch'en Ti attempted to define ancient phonetics by classifying and comparing rhyme words in the Book of Songs.[45] His method in phonetical research was later adopted by the early Ch'ing scholar, Ku Yen-wu.[46] Chiao Hung rejected orthodox commentaries and interpretations of the classics, arguing that they sometimes obscured the true meanings of the classics. He, therefore, suggested that scholars go back directly to the classics without first referring to the commentaries. He advocated a linguistic or philological approach

---

[44]P'i, op. cit., p. 202. See also Chan, "Chu Hsi's Completion of Neo-Confucianism", pp. 132-134; James T. C. Liu, Ou-yang Hsiu: An Eleventh-Century Neo-Confucianist (Stanford: Stanford University Press, 1967), p. 94 and Elman, "The Unravelling of Neo-Confucianism", pp. 83-85.

[45]Elman, "The Unravelling of Neo-Confucianism", pp. 88, 387-388.

[46]See ECCP, v. 1, pp. 421-426.

to the classics.[47] These reorientations in classical scholarship anticipated and laid the ground-work for later developments in evidential research in early Ch'ing times.

During the seventeenth century, Ku Yen-wu, Yen Jo-chü 閻若璩 (1636-1704)[48] and others reacted vigorously against the orthodox classical scholarship of the Ming, which had been philosophical in its approach and created a new climate of learning as well as a new mode of thought, thus more scholarly in nature.[49] They emphasized the study of the classics based on textual research and extensive evidence. Yen Jo-chü exhibited a strong spirit of skepticism in his critical examinations of the ancient texts. His major achievement as a classical scholar is the Shang-shu ku-wen shu-cheng 尚書古文疏證 (Evidential Analysis of the Ancient Text [Version of the] Book of History). While the authenticity of the Book of History, which had been studied by scholars for ages, had been questioned by scholars before Yen's time, it was generally accepted as a valid work. Yen employed empirical methods to analyze the text, and based on extensive philological evidence concluded that the Ancient Text chapters were a

---

[47]See Edward T. Ch'ien, "Chiao Hung and the Revolt against Ch'eng-Chu Orthodoxy" in Wm. Theodore de Bary, ed., The Unfolding of Neo-Confucianism (New York: Columbia University Press, 1975), pp. 287-291 and his Chiao Hung and the Restructuring of Neo-Confucianism in the Late Ming (New York: Columbia University Press, 1986), pp. 181-182.

[48]ECCP, v. 2, pp. 908-910.

[49]Elman, From Philosophy to Philology, pp. 43-44.

later forgery. This conclusion was later accepted by most k'ao-cheng scholars of the time.[50]

Another important figure was Ku Yen-wu. Ku is generally regarded as the founder of the school of evidential research, for he developed a new research methodology. Although the main purpose of his study was the practical application of knowledge to society, Ku did stress that textual criticism and philological investigation were indispensable for the study of the classics, and defined research methods appropriate to the various branches of study. Thus, the research methodologies which Ku originated, did signal a reorientation in classical scholarship and paved the way for the rise of the k'ao-cheng school in mid-Ch'ing times.[51] The term k'ao-cheng was not a neologism; instead it was a term which had been used by the Sung scholar Wang Ying-lin 王應麟 (1223-1296). However, it only came into vogue during the seventeenth century.[52]

Ch'ing scholars turned to k'ao-cheng scholarship for several reasons. Modern Chinese scholars have tended to attribute the rise of k'ao-cheng scholarship to the oppressive rule and literary inquisitions of an alien government, which sought to prohibit all political discussions which it believed might endanger

---

[50]ECCP, v. 2, pp. 909-910.

[51]ECCP, v. 1, pp. 423-424.

[52]Elman, From Philosophy to Philology, p. 45.

the state.[53] In order to avoid becoming involved in the repressive actions by the government, scholars tended to shy away from political and social affairs. Instead, they turned to classical studies as a safe haven from political oppression. While similar persecutions had been implemented from time to time during the previous dynasty, what came to be known as k'ao-cheng scholarship did not emerge as a distinct phenomena until the seventeenth century.[54]

Another reason, for the emergence of the new scholarship was that it represented a rejection of the rigidities of orthodox Neo-Confucianism.[55] With the fall of the Ming dynasty in 1644, some early Ch'ing scholars concluded that the abstract speculative philosophy of Sung-Ming Neo-Confucianism was largely responsible for the collapse of the dynasty,[56] for it had become remote from the concrete day-to-day problems of society. Influential individuals like Ch'ien Ch'ien-i

---

[53]For the link between Manchu repressive policies and k'ao-cheng scholarship, see Liang, op. cit., p. 47, and T'ang Chih-chün 湯志鈞 , "Ch'ing-tai Ch'ang-chou ching chin-wen hsüeh-p'ai yü wu-hsü pien-fa 清代常州經今文學派與戊戌變法 " in Wu-hsü pien-fa shih lun-ts'ung 戊戌變法史論叢 (Hong Kong: Ch'ung-wen shu-tien, 1973), p. 74.

[54]Elman, From Philosophy to Philology, pp. 14-17. See also Susan Mann Jones, "Scholasticism and Politics in Late Eighteenth Century China" Ch'ing-shih wen-t'i, 3:4 (Dec., 1975), pp. 28-29. See also Lawrence Kessler, "Chinese Scholars and the Early Manchu State," Harvard Journal of Asiatic Studies 31 (1971), pp. 179-200; Hellmut Wilhelm, "The Po-hsüeh Hung-ju Examination of 1679," Journal of the American Oriental Society 71 (1951), pp. 60-66; and Luther C. Goodrich, The Literary Inquisition of Ch'ien-lung (Baltimore: Waverly Press, 1935).

[55]See for example, Liang, op. cit., p. 21.

[56]Elman, From Philosophy to Philology, p. 50.

錢謙益 (b. 1630) and Ku Yen-wu, for instance, advocated the pursuit of knowledge for practical use, and stressed a return to the classics, as compared to the Sung dynasty commentaries, as the means of discovering the truth of the sages. They also asserted that Sung-Ming Neo-Confucianism suffered from two basic weaknesses: first, it was contaminated by Buddhist and Taoist ideas; and second, the Sung-Ming philosphers' inadequacies, their lack of proper philological training, caused them to base themselves on incorrect and incomplete readings of the Confucian texts.[57] To examine, refine, and correct the perceived errors of the Sung-Ming Neo-Confucianists, the proponents of k'ao-cheng scholarship favored a return to the past in order to recover the authentic texts, and thus the truths of original Confucianism. In the process they turned toward philology and away from philosophy.[58]

While both interpretations - those of political pressure and scholarly reaction against Neo-Confucianism orthodoxy - were perhaps contributing factors, any explanation of such intellectual movement as k'ao-cheng scholarship should not overlook certain factors inherent in the development of Confucianism. Recent studies have shown that k'ao-cheng scholarship was a continuation rather than a

---

[57]Yü Ying-shih, "Some Preliminary Observations on the Rise of Ch'ing Confucian Intellectualism", Tsing Hua Journal of Chinese Studies, v. 11 (1975), p. 112.

[58]By philosophy, Ch'ing scholars meant metaphysical and cosmological systems of thought.

discontinuation of Sung-Ming Neo-Confucianism. Yü Ying-shih, in particular, has argued that Ch'ing philology can be understood as inherent in the development of Sung-Ming Neo-Confucianism.[59] While all of these interpretations, these discussions of internal and external factors, served to deepen our understanding of these momentous shifts in intellectual perspective, the most important factor leading to the rise and eventual prevalence of k'ao-cheng scholarship was changes in the social and academic environment of the time.[60]

During the Ch'ing dynasty, with an increase in the number of degree-holders relative to the size of the bureaucratic structure, winning one of the higher degrees seldom guaranteed an official career. Thus, unlike their predecessors in earlier times, Ch'ing scholars tended to become specialists in k'ao-cheng scholarship rather than become scholar-officials.[61] This tendency was possible chiefly because of patronage through government, provincial officials and merchants. With this patronage, scholars not only could make their own living but also could carry out their k'ao-cheng research. Due to official and semiofficial patronage, k'ao-cheng scholarship flourished during the eighteenth century. Such patronage

---

[59]Yü, op. cit., p. 128.

[60]Tu, op. cit., pp. 117-118.

[61]Elman, From Philosophy to Philology, pp. 95, 130.

came in the form of literary projects, public and private.[62] Private scholars were appointed to the secretarial staffs (mu-yu) of provincial and local officials, where some were employed in academic projects. In that way classical and historical texts were edited and local gazetteers were compiled. Merchants also played an important role in the promotion of k'ao-cheng scholarship and were great patrons of the literary and historical arts and well as the benefactors of academies and schools.

Scholars not only participated in a wide variety of literary projects, they were also employed as teachers in schools or academies, and there, too, were able to persue individual research interests. The existence of numerous private libraries -- some of considerable size and scope -- and printing houses also served to foster the spread of the new scholarship. During the eighteenth century, books were compiled, printed, and made available for purchase in numbers much greater than ever before. The growth of large, private libraries paticularly in Kiangnan, and the publication of a great diversity of books, classical and modern, made printed scholarship and reference materials accessible to a growing readership. In addition, new and improved means of scholarly communications, including notation books to share research techniques, scholarly collaboration, as well as correspondence and meetings of individual scholar, played an important role in the

---

[62]Over 150 separate research projects were sponsored by the government. For the comprehensive list of these projects, see Tu, op. cit., pp. 120-130.

advancement of k'ao-cheng scholarship during the eighteenth century. The total social and academic environment which developed in Ch'ing times was thus crucial to the emergence, maintenance and advancement of k'ao-cheng scholarship.[63]

K'ao-cheng scholars, as has been indicated before, based their studies of the ancient classics on pre-Sung dynasty texts, namely, those of the Han, for they favored the fu-ku 復古 (return to the past) orientation, which represented an attempt to rediscover the essentials of Confucian belief. Han dynasty texts and commentaries, they believed, were more reliable, more authentic because they were closer in time to antiquity and therefore to truth. Since the eighteenth century, evidential scholarship focused on the textual annotations by Han scholars and employed research methods first developed during that time, evidential scholarship was designated Han Learning.[64]

Ch'ing evidential scholars of the Han Learning school modelled themselves on Cheng Hsüan who had combined the New and Ancient Text persuasions in his annotations of the classics. Thus, individuals who adopted that outlook represented a mixture of both the Ancient and New Text scholarships.[65] Modern scholars have tended to the belief that Cheng Hsüan belonged to the Ancient Text

---

[63]For the social and academic environment created by the Ch'ing, see Elman, From Philosophy to Philology, pp. 100-204.

[64]Liang, op. cit., pp. 86-88.

[65]Lu, op. cit., pp. 92-98. See also Chiang, op. cit., p. 23.

School, and that the evidential research school of mid-Ch'ing times was, therefore, an adherent of the Ancient Text School.[66] However, this was not necessarily the case, for one tenet of k'ao-cheng scholarship was that interpretations of the classics must be based on solid textual evidence, and in evaluating the evidence at hand, the most ancient texts were preferred. Therefore, on the basis of evidence deriving from the Former and Later Han, k'ao-cheng scholars were prepared to reject Sung dynasty interpretations of the classics.[67] This was obvious in Hui Tung's 惠棟 (1697-1758)[68] and Tai Chen's 戴震 (1724-1777)[69] respective approaches to learning. Hui Tung was recognized as the founder of the so-called Wu, or Soochow School, and the fundamental spirit of his approach to learning was "that which is ancient must be authentic and that which is of the Han must be good."[70] He even attempted to elevate the views of the Han masters to

---

[66]See Liang, op. cit., p. 87. See also Chang Hao, Liang Ch'i-ch'ao and Intellectual Transition in China, 1890-1907 (Berkeley: University of California Press, 1987), p. 21.

[67]Liang, op. cit., p. 67.

[68]ECCP, v. 1, pp. 357-358.

[69]Ibid., v. 2, pp. 695-700. On Tai Chen, consult Ch'eng Chung-ying, Tai Chen's Inquiry into Goodness (Honolulu: East-West Center Press, 1971) and Hu Shih 胡適, Tai Tung-yüan te che-hsüeh 戴東原的哲學 (Taipei: Commerical Press, 1967).

[70]See quote in Liang, op. cit., p. 53.

48

the rank of classics.[71] Because he so revered the Han scholars, there was little or no reason for him to reject the New Text School and to favor the Ancient Text School.

Tai Chen, regarded by many as the greatest thinker and scholar of the Ch'ing era, stated that the aim of k'ao-cheng scholarship was to get at the Confucian truth. His approach to scholarship was to seek the truth by investigating the facts without favoring any one school.[72] Thus, his approach to the classics was different from that of Hui Tung. Although Tai respected the scholarship of the Han scholars, he was opposed to following it blindly.[73] Since his methods were objective in nature, he sought to eliminate any bias against the New Text School. Under the influence of these two great scholars, Tai Chen and Hui Tung, their followers made it their purpose to discover the philosophical verities of the ancient texts through the gathering of textual evidence by means of a rigorous methodology. Thus, in selecting classical texts for annotation, they did not limit themselves to the ancient Confucian texts only.[74]

The late Ch'ing master of Han Learning, Yü Yüeh passed on to his students, including Chang Ping-lin, knowledge of its goals and methodologies. Since Chang

---

[71]Ibid., pp. 52-53.

[72]Ibid., p. 57.

[73]Ibid., pp. 56-57.

[74]Chiang, op. cit., p. 23.

Ping-lin spent seven years in the academy where Yü Yüeh was the master, he received a solid grounding in that discipline. Afterwards, Han Learning formed the foundation of his scholarship and remained a lifelong devotion. And because of his mentor's influence, Chang's intellectual tendency at this time was also characterized by including the scholarships of these two schools. This was evident in his articles published in the journal of the academy, Ku-ching ching-she k'e-i 詁經精舍課藝 (Collected School Works of the Ku-ching Academy). In some of these articles, Chang also adopted ideas from the New Text School.[75] Although Chang claimed to be an advocate of the Ancient Text School in 1891,[76] he did not at that time reject New Text ideas. Even after he left the academy and joined the staff of the Shih-wu pao 時務報 (Current Affairs Journal) in 1897, he still continued to utilize New Text concepts and beliefs in articles written for that journal.[77] However, he later started openly to criticize the views of New Text scholars. It was not because Chang was an Ancient Text proponent as such that he did so, but because, according to his own testimony, they had distorted history for political purposes.[78] As he observed, if history could be distorted, "there is

---

[75]NPCP, v. 1, p. 19.

[76]TTNP, pp. 4-5.

[77]NPCP, v. 1, pp. 40-42.

[78]Wang, op. cit., pp. 51-52.

no word in history that can be trusted."[79] As an advocate of k'ao-cheng tenets, he followed wholeheartedly the principle, "to get at the truth through concrete facts and to hold no belief without evidence".[80] Therefore, Chang stated that he could not endure distortions of history. His refutation of the views of the New Text scholars did not, however, represent a revival of the dispute between the New Text and Ancient Text schools.

During his years at the academy, Chang's writings which were published in the school journal represented textual commentaries on the Confucian classics. Apart from his study of those texts, he also devoted considerable attention to the study of the ancient noncanonical texts, the so-called chu-tzu hsüeh 諸子學 .[81] Chang compiled four volumes of study notes, the Kao-lan-shih cha-chi 膏蘭室 札記 (Study Notes Written in the Kao-lan Studio), wherein most of the entries represented textual commentaries on noncanonical texts. His interest in the study of both Confucian and non-Confucian texts of the Chou era was undoubtedly influenced by his teacher, Yü Yüeh, who combined the studies of both in his teaching at the academy.[82] This interest in the study of the ancient noncanonical

---

[79]Chang, "Chin-ku-wen pien-yi" 今古文辨義 , in CLHC, v. 1, p. 115.

[80]See quote in Liang, op. cit., p. 24.

[81]The chu-tzu hsüeh refers to ancient noncannonical texts dating from the Warring States Period (403-221 B.C.), or earlier, but excludes the Confucian texts by Confucius and Mencius.

[82]Wang, op. cit., pp. 24-25.

texts was not a local phenomenon, but instead represented a key feature of late Ch'ing scholarship. This revival was, in fact, rooted in k'ao-cheng scholarship.[83] The aim of mid-Ch'ing k'ao-cheng scholarship was to recover the original Confucian truth through a rigorous study of the ancient classics. Therefore, these scholars favored a return to the past in order to recover the authentic truth of original Confucianism. From this impetus, there resulted a revival of the exegetical scholarship of Han times. And in seeking corroborating evidence for their textual studies, these scholars turned to pre-Ch'in noncanonical texts, sources closer in time to the Confucian classics than the Han scholars.[84]

Another factor that contributed to the revival of the classical noncanonical texts was the collation of ancient texts. One contribution to classical studies made by Ch'ing scholars was collating ancient texts. Since the majority of the collated texts were those of the pre-Ch'in noncanonical texts, this, therefore, stimulated Ch'ing scholars' interest in the study of pre-Ch'in noncanonical texts.[85]

During the late Ch'ing, research of this kind flourished, with the result that reliable, modern editions of such texts as the Mo-tzu 墨子 were established. Yü

---

[83]Ibid., p. 26.

[84]For a discussion of the growing scholarly interest in the reexamination of the ancient noncannonical texts, see Ibid., pp. 26-27. See also Chang Hao, Chinese Intellectuals in Crisis, pp. 10-11.

[85]Liang, op. cit., pp. xxxiv-xxxvii. See also Elman, From Philosophy to Philology, p. 76.

Yüeh, for instance, wrote textual commentaries on several classical noncanonical texts.

Yü Yüeh regarded the classical noncanonical texts and the Confucian classics as being equally important in understanding the ancient past; therefore, he elevated his Chu-tzu p'ing-i 諸子平議 (Fair Evaluations of the Classical Noncanonical Texts) to the same rank of his Ch'ün-ching p'ing-i 群經平議 (Fair Evaluation of the Assembled Classics). Under the influence of Yü Yüeh, Chang Ping-lin also affirmed the value of the ancient non-canonical texts.[86] In fact, those texts came in time to exert a great influence on Chang's thinking.

Chang's intellectual interests were not confined to indigenous scholarship, but went beyond the boundaries of China's cultural heritage. In fact, beginning in the early 1890s, he came in contact with Western learning. His attitude toward Western learning reflected one of the important intellectual trends of his time, that is, the attempt to fit Western ideas into the existing framework of traditional Chinese culture. This tendency had changed little since China's acceptance of Western learning in the mid-nineteenth century.[87]

---

[86]Wang, op. cit., p. 29.

[87]Ch'üan Han-sheng 全漢昇 , "Ch'ing-mo te ʻHsi-hsüeh ch'u Chung- kuo' shuo" 清末的西學出中國說 , in Li Ting-i 李定一 et al., Chung-kuo chin-tai-shih lun-ts'ung 中國近代史論叢 (Taipei: Cheng-chung shu-chü, 1966), series 1, vol. 5, pp. 216-258. See also Chow Tse-tsung, "The Anti-Confucian Movement in Early Republican China", in Arthur F. Wright, ed., The Confucian Persuasion, pp. 288-289.

Although Western learning was first introduced into China by Catholic missionaries from Europe during the Ming-Ch'ing transitional era, Western learning was largely ignored until the 1860s.[88] Even after China was defeated in the Opium War of 1839-1842 by Great Britain, this humiliating experience failed to awaken most Chinese to the realities of their own deficiencies and the persistent threat of foreign aggression. Subsequently, China encountered the dual crisis of internal rebellion and external invasion, and these problems eventually became too pervasive for the Chinese any longer to ignore. The vast internal upheavels which troubled China in the mid-nineteenth century included, among others, the Taiping Rebellion (1850-1864) in the south and south-central provinces, the Nien Rebellion (1851-1868) in north-central China, and the Moslem Rebellions-- one (1855-1873) in the extreme southwest and another (1862-1873) in the northwest. These rebellions seriously weakened the social and political infrastructure, and increased Chinese vulnerability to external threat. The external crisis involved a long series of military defeats began with the Opium Wars and continued through the Boxer catastrophe; all of them humiliated China and threatened her with extinction from external aggression.[89] From the 1860s to 1890s, when the national crisis deepened, some Chinese officials and scholars became convinced that in order

---

[88]Immanuel C. Y. Hsü, The Rise of Modern China (New York: Oxford University Press, 1975), p. 261.

[89]Ibid.

to resist foreign aggression and to suppress domestic rebellion, China must acquire knowledge of modern military technology from the West. Thus, the effort to gain Western learning at this time emphasized science and technology.[90] However, after China was defeated in the Sino-Japanese War of 1894-1895, some Chinese officials and scholars realized that what China needed if it was to survive was not only Western science and technology, but also modern political institutions, laws and philosophical ideas.[91] Thus, before 1895, Chinese interest in Western learning focused mostly on technical information (i 藝), while after 1895, interest in the West broadened to include political institutions (cheng 政) and philosophical as well as religious ideas (chiao 教).[92] Different as the scope of its acceptance of Western learning was before and after 1895, the Chinese attitude toward Western learning changed only slowly over time. And the importation of new ideas often required sanction by claiming that Western learning had its origin in traditional Chinese scholarship, or that these Western ideas could also be found in Chinese classics.[93]

---

[90]Ibid., p. 420.

[91]Ibid., p. 421.

[92]Chang Hao, "Intellectual Change and the Reform Movement, 1890-8, p. 275.

[93]Chow, "The Anti-Confucian Movement in Early Republican China", pp. 288-289.

In the intellectual climate of the time, Chang's scholarly attention was not exclusively concentrated on traditional Chinese scholarship. Actually, he probably began to study Western science in 1891.[94] In his study notes, the Kao-lan-shih cha-chi, compiled between 1891 and 1893, we find him borrowing ideas from Western science in commenting on the Chinese classics. For instance, in seeking to elucidate the "series of ten points" of Hui Shih 惠施 (fl. 370-310 B.C.) as preserved in the "T'ien-hsia" 天下 (The World) chapter of the Chuang-tzu 莊子 , Chang cites Euclid's Geometric Principles.[95] However, his acceptance of Western learning was not without reservation. Like his contemporaries, his attitude toward Western learning at this time was to claim that the concepts of Western science were all to be found in the Chinese classics.[96] Nevertheless, Western learning still had a significant influence on his later thinking, especially on the formation of his concept of kuo-ts'ui.

The late nineteenth century also witnessed a revival of interest in Mahayana Buddhism, which was stimulated in large part by a layman, Yang Wen-hui 楊文會(1837-1911).[97] Many of Chang's contemporaries took an interest in Buddhist

---

[94]Ho Ch'eng-hsüan 何成軒 , Chang Ping-lin te che-hsüeh ssu-hsiang 章炳麟的哲學思想 (Hupei: Jen-min ch'u-pan she, 1987), p. 64.

[95]CTYCC, v. 1, pp. 243-247.

[96]Ibid., v. 1, p. 197.

[97]Holmes Welch, The Buddhist Revival in China (Cambridge: Harvard University Press, 1968), pp. 1-2.

concepts, such as T'an Ssu-t'ung 譚嗣同 (1865-1898).[98] Although in his middle

age Chang's father revealed a fondness for the study of Ch'an Buddhism,[99]

Chang himself showed no interest in such beliefs until he came to know Hsia

Tseng-yu 夏曾佑 (1863-1924), who introduced him to such Buddhist sutras as the

Saddharma pundarika Sutra (the Lotus Sutra), the Avatamsaka Sutra (Garland

Sutra), and the Nirvana Sutra. Although he read these famous texts, it is unlikely

he comprehended them fully or found them very convincing.[100] Later in 1897,

he was also persuaded to study the works of the Three-Treatise School by a close

friend, Sung Shu 宋恕 (1862-1910). However, after he finished reading these

texts, it appears that his attitude toward Buddhism remained largely negative.[101]

It is no surprise that Chang had no lasting interest in Buddhism. His

philosophical and scholarly interests at that time were centered on Confucianism,

especially on Hsün Tzu, and he tended to regard Buddhism in largely traditional

---

[98]ECCP, v. 2, pp. 702-705. On T'an Ssu-t'ung, see Chan Sin-wai, Buddhism in Late Ch'ing Political Thought (Hong Kong: The Chinese University Press, 1985), pp. 53-134.

[99]T'ang Wen-ch'üan 唐文權 and Lo Fu-hui 羅福惠 , Chang T'ai-yen ssu-hsiang yen-chiu 章太炎思想研究 (Wu-ch'ang: Hua-chung shih-fan ta-hsüeh ch'u-pan she, 1986), p. 239.

[100]TTNP, p. 5.

[101]Ibid., pp. 5-6. These three treatises are the Madhyamika sastra (Treatise on the Middle Doctrine), the Dvadasanikayasastra (Twelve Gates Treatise) and the Satasastra (One Hundred Verses Treatise).

Confucian terms as empty talk.[102] Although he criticized Buddhist teachings by claiming that they were impractical, he still affirmed the value of studying the Buddhist religion for its importance to the history of both northwestern China and Central Asia.[103] Thus, while Chang read Buddhist texts during his mid-twenties, he did not become an earnest student of Buddhist philosophy until he was imprisoned in Shanghai from 1903 to 1906.[104] Thereafter, it continued to exercise a great influence on his later intellectual development.

Thus, by the time Chang left the Ku-ching Academy in 1896 to join the staff of the reform journal, the Shih-wu pao 時務報 (Current Affairs Journal), which had been founded earlier that same year by Liang Ch'i-ch'ao (1873-1929) and Hsia Tseng-yu,[105] Chang had been exposed to a broad range of philosophical and intellectual influences, both native and foreign. Among them, Han Learning formed the foundation of his perceptions and scholarly interests and encouraged him to widen his intellectual interests, especially with respect to long neglected aspects of his own tradition. And in time, he became a devoted student of Chinese classical scholarship.

---

[102]Ibid., p. 6.

[103]Wang, op. cit., p. 37.

[104]TTNP, p. 10.

[105]Ibid., p. 5. See also Feng, op. cit., v. 1, p. 112.

CHAPTER 3

CHANG PING-LIN AND "NATIONAL ESSENCE"

Although Chang Ping-lin is well-known for his role in the revolutionary movement that culminated in the termination of imperial rule in 1911, he is more often remembered as a prominent classical scholar. His life and thought illustrates the uneasy relationship between political revolution and cultural conservatism among the intellectuals of his generation, and his advocacy of preserving the national essence paved the way for the far-reaching National Essence Movement in the early twentieth century.

As a revolutionary, Chang called for the preservation of the national essence. His emphasis on the national essence clearly distinguished him from most of the other intellectuals in the revolutionary movement.[1] Most intellectuals of his time concerned themselves not with the protection of the traditional culture but with the political entity of the nation. While Chang was also concerned with the survival of the nation, he perceived the nation not only as a political entity but also as a cultural entity. Thus, while he was concerned about the search for national wealth and power, his ultimate concern or goal was protecting the traditional culture from extinction from external forces. This commitment to the preservation of the national essence was the most fundamental and constant characteristic of

---

[1]See Michael Gasster, <u>Chinese Intellectuals and the Revolution of 1911</u>, p. 201.

his thinking. This chapter will illustrate Chang's effort to preserve the national essence, and analyze the origins of Chang's concept of the national essence, as well as its scope and meaning.

Chang's Concern for the Preservation of the National Essence

Although Chang Ping-lin became a reformer in the 1890s who later supported the revolution wholeheartedly, the effort to preserve China's national essence was the most important mission in his life. Chang's devotion to these political activities was largely a means to protect China's cultural heritage and to assure its continuity. Even during his careers as a reformist and a revolutionist, he devoted most of his time and energies to teaching and to classical scholarship, and to publishing a number of his most important works on Chinese classical studies. He also expressed repeatedly the crucial need to perpetuate the national essence, and to that end, he established private schools and seminars, a literary society, and published scholarly magazines.

Chang's concern to preserve the national essence was not only because he was a classical scholar, and therefore, assumed the responsibility of upholding classical teachings, but also because he believed it was essential for the survival of the nation. He even claimed that there were people who could make the same contribution to the promotion of the Chinese revolutionary movement as he did. However, no one could be compared with him for contributing to the preservation of China's national essence. He stated it very clearly when he was in prison in

June, 1903, for the Su-pao (Kiangsu Daily) case (Su-pao an　蘇報案　)[2]:

> I am endowed with [the talent to preserve] the national essence from
> Heaven. In the thirty-six years since my birth the male phoenix has
> not come and the Yellow River has not brought forth a map, and I
> hold no official position either. Nevertheless, I still follow the
> teachings of the uncrowned king. How can I be a stickler for ancient
> ways and things? Instead, I will devote my talent to enhance and
> glorify the national essence. However, after I had been imprisoned
> in a hostile country, I could not have my wish fulfilled to promote the
> national essence. [Under this circumstance], there are people who
> can still carry on the unfinished task of revolution. But, as to China's
> grand and splendid learning, it would then not continue [after the
> revolution]. Thus, it would be my fault, if the national heritage and
> customs would become extinct in my own hands.[3]

Chang also asserted, "after I died, Chinese culture would be extinguished."[4] Thus,

he later asserted that his life-long commitment was "to revere Chinese history and

preserve China's unique spoken and written languages,"[5] for he believed, "the

---

[2]For more details of the Su-pao case, see chapter 4.

[3]Chang, "K'ui-mao yü-chung tzu-chi"　癸卯獄中自記　, in CTYCC, v. 4, p. 144.
In this passage, male phoenix (fang-niao 鳳鳥) is a kind of fabulous bird, which
is said to appear when a sage ascends to the throne or when right principles are
going to triumph in the world. The Yellow River Map (ho-t'u 河圖) is originated
with Fu Hsi 伏羲 , a legendary ruler of China, and is a symbol of divine thing.
That it appears implies the sage will rule the world. See The Four Books, tr.,
James Legge (Taipei: Tun-huang shu-chü, n.d.), pp. 111-112.

[4]See "Chang T'ai-yen hsien-sheng chia-shu"　章太炎先生家書　, Appendix to
CSTS, v. 2, p. 24.

[5]See Chu Tsu-keng 朱祖耿 , "Chi pen-shih Chang-kung tzu-shu chih-hsüeh
chih kung-fu chi chih-hsiang" 記本師章公自述治學之功夫及志向, Chih-yen 制言 25
(Sept. 16, 1936), p. 6.

differences among nations are their histories as well as their spoken and written languages[6], which became two of the key attributes of Chang's kuo-ts'ui concept. He sought to protect these characteristics, especially when China was under the pressure from foreign powers.

After his release from prison on June 29, 1906, Chang was accompanied to Japan by four members of the newly founded Revolutionary Alliance (T'ung-meng hui 同盟會), a united revolutionary organization, which had been founded on August 20, 1905.[7] Later, on July 15, Chang was asked to make a speech at a welcoming party, which was held in Tokyo in his honor.[8] In this speech, Chang did not talk about such aspects as politics, law, and military affairs, which, he said, were not necessary to discuss at that moment, for most of his audience had already studied all these subjects. Instead, Chang stressed kuo-ts'ui in his speech.[9] Chang maintained that, in order to overthrow the Manchu dynasty, it was necessary "to employ kuo-ts'ui to stimulate racial character (chung-

---

[6]Ibid.

[7]NPCP, v. 1, pp. 200, 210.

[8]TTNP, p. 11. Chang himself says that seven thousand people attended his speech.

[9]See Chang, "Wo te p'ing-sheng yü pan-shih fang-fa" 我的平生與辦事方法 , in Chang T'ai-yen te pai-hua wen 章太炎的白話文 (Taipei: I-wen yin-shu kuan, 1972), p. 91. See also Gasster, op. cit., p. 201.

hsing 種性) and to promote patriotic fervor."[10] However, Chang claimed, "To promote kuo-ts'ui does not mean that people should believe in Confucianism as a religion, but it means that people should value the history of Han Chinese."[11] Chang's talk, which emphasized the kuo-ts'ui, certainly was contrary to the expectations of most of his audience. The majority, who were new to the revolutionary movement, had anticipated that Chang's speech would recount his experiences in the attack upon the Manchus and talk about his knowledge of western law and politics, which, after the successful revolution, could contribute to the building of a new China that resembled Western nations in many ways.[12] Nevertheless, Chang was invited to join the T'ung-meng hui. His appointment as editor-in-chief of the Min-pao 民報 (People's Journal), the official organ of the T'ung-meng hui, was due to his eminence as a classical scholar and his fame arising from the Su-pao case.[13] Before Chang took over the editorship, Min-pao had wrestled with K'ang-Liang reformers over political ideology and over the

---

[10]Chang, "Wo te p'ing-sheng yü pan-shih fang-fa", p. 91.

[11]Ibid., p. 96.

[12]See Gasster, op. cit., pp. 201-202.

[13]TTNP, p. 11. Also see BDRC, v. 1, p. 94. Min-pao put out the first issue on November 26, 1905. Until it was suspended by the Japanese authorities on October 10, 1908, twenty-four issues were published. Chang began his editorship of the journal on September 5, 1906, and edited fourteen issues during these two years. See NPCP, v. 1, p. 207.

support from the overseas Chinese.[14] Although Chang was a spokesman for the rising revolutionary movement, his <u>Min-pao</u> articles did not strongly attack K'ang-Liang's rationale for protecting the <u>Kuang-hsü</u> emperor (r. 1875-1908) or their reform ideas, but dealt mostly with the preservation of the Chinese national essence.[15] He even criticized the views of Hu Han-min 胡漢民　(1879-1936) and Wang Ching-wei 汪精衛　(1883-1944) because their <u>Min-pao</u> articles attacked Liang Ch'i-ch'ao too bitterly.[16]

During his 1906-1908 editorship, Chang was also the most prolific contributor to the <u>Min-pao</u>. He published about sixty-eight articles in this journal.[17] The chief editor Chang, even changed the <u>Min-pao</u> from a popular radical organ into something almost as scholarly as <u>The National Essence Journal</u> (<u>kuo-ts'ui hsüeh-pao</u> 國粹學報　) founded in 1905 by Liu Shih-p'ei 劉師培

---

[14]<u>NPCP</u>, v. 1, pp. 223-225. See also Wong Young-tsu, <u>Search for Modern Nationalism</u>, p. 48.

[15]See "Hu Han-min tzu-chuan" 胡漢民自傳　 in <u>Ko-ming wen-hsien</u> 革命文獻 (Taipei: Kuo-min-tang tang-shih hui, 1953), v. 3, p. 390. Also see Chu Hung-yüan 朱浤源　, "Min-pao chung te Chang T'ai-yen" 民報中的章太炎 <u>Ta-lu tsa-chih</u> 大陸雜誌　68:2 (Feb. 15, 1984), p. 68.

[16]<u>TTNP</u>, p. 11.

[17]See Chu Hung-yüan, <u>T'ung-meng hui te ke-ming li-lun</u> 同盟會的革命理論 (Taipei: Chung-yang yen-chiu-yüan chin-tai shih yen-chiu so, 1985), pp. 339-341.

(1884-1919).[18] Chang was also a contributor to the National Essence Journal

and was later involved in the National Essence Movement, a culturally conservative

movement.

Aside from editing the Min-pao, Chang devoted his time to teaching and

research on Chinese national studies (kuo-hsüeh 國學). In September, 1906,

Chang had organized the Seminar for National Studies (Kuo-hsüeh chiang-hsi hui

國學講習會) to promote the national essence.[19] Its preamble provided a useful

reference to Chang's concern and the ideas he propounded in the Min-pao period:

> National Studies is the basis for founding the nation. I hear that in
> this competing world, it is insufficient to establish a nation by its
> national studies only, however, I never heard that a nation can be [
> established] independently without promoting its national studies; I
> hear that there are nations which have been perished but their
> national studies are not extinct. However, I never heard that a nation
> whose national studies had been extinguished could still exist. Thus,
> if no one arises to promote national studies, it will lead to the
> downfall of the nation.[20]

The seminar was to serve Chang's goal: He claimed that preserving Chinese

culture was essential for the survival of the nation. Chang gave a lecture at Ta-

ch'eng high school in Tokyo twice a week. Some of Chang's most talented

---

[18]See Martin Bernal, "Liu Shih-pei and National Essence" in Charlotte Furth, ed., The Limits of Change: Essays on Conservative Alternatives in Republican China (Cambridge: Harvard University Press, 1976), pp. 104, 109.

[19]See Sung Chiao-jen 宋教仁 , Sung Chiao-jen jih-chi 宋教仁日記 (Ch'ang-sha: Hunan jen-min ch'u-pan she, 1980), p. 249.

[20]Min-pao, no. 7 (Sept. 5, 1906), p. 26.

students, such as, Lu Hsün 魯迅 (1881-1936), Chu Hsi-tsu 朱希祖 (1879-1944)

and Huang K'an 黃侃 (1886-1936), who later became distinguished writers and

scholars, attended Chang's special Seminar. Chang did not abolish the Seminar

until the Wu-ch'ang 武昌 Uprising in 1911.[21] Chang also established a literary

society, Kuo-hsüeh chen-ch'i-she 國學振起社 (the Society for the Promotion

of National Studies), the aim of which was "to promote national studies and to

enhance national glory (Kuo-kuang 國光)".[22] In advocating the national

essence, Chang also published a number of his most important works on Chinese

traditional learning from 1906 to 1910.[23]

The effort to promote study of the past remained central to Chang's life after

1911. In 1913, Chang re-established the Seminar for National Studies in Peking

when he was placed under house arrest by Yüan Shih-K'ai 袁世凱 (1859-1916).[24]

In 1923, Chang edited a scholarly magazine, Hua-kuo 華國 (The Splendid

---

[21]See NPCP, v. 1, pp. 289-295. Also see Hsü Shou-shang 許壽裳 , Chang Ping-lin 章炳麟 (Nanking: Sheng-li ch'u-pan kung-ssu, 1945), pp. 78-79.

[22]NPCP, v. 1, p. 217. See also Chiang, op. cit., p. 428.

[23]They are: Ch'un-chiu Tso-chuan tu hsü-lu 春秋左傳讀敍錄 , Hsin fang-yen 新方言 , Chuang-tzu chieh-ku 莊子解故 , Wen-shih 文始 , Kuo-ku lun-heng 國故論衡 , Ch'i-wu-lun shih 齊物論釋 , Liu Tzu-cheng Tso-shih shuo 劉子政左氏說 , and Hsiao-hsüeh ta-wen 小學答問

[24]See NPCP, v. 2, pp. 455-456; Chiang, op. cit., pp. 592-593; Wang Yu-wei 王有爲, Chang T'ai-yen chuan 章太炎傳 (Kuangtung: Jen-min ch'u-pan she, 1984), pp. 144-145.

66

Country), in which he published a number of his classical studies.[25] In 1935, Chang set up a permanent type of seminar, Chang's Seminar for National Studies (Chang-shih kuo-hsüeh chiang-hsi-hui 章氏國學講習會) in Soochow (Su-chou). Its aim was "to study the traditional Chinese culture and to educate men of talent with the discipline of national studies".[26] Chang also published a semi-monthly magazine, Chih-yen (Model Sayings), as its organ. Chang spent the last two years before his death on June 14, 1936, in teaching at the seminar.[27] Thus, through writings published in these journals, the establishment of a literary society, and the lectures at these seminars, Chang continued to serve his goal, protecting China's national culture.

Chang's publicist contributions to the revolution continued. After the Min-pao was suspended by Japanese authorities in 1908, Chang, in 1910, became the editor of the Journal of New Comments on Education (Chiao-yü chin-yü tsa-chih 教育今語雜誌), an organ of the Restoration Society (Kuang-fu hui 光復會),

---

[25]See NPCP, v. 2, p. 727; BDRC, v. 1, p. 96. The journal was founded in Shanghai on September 15, 1923.

[26]NPCP, v. 2, p. 960; Also see Shen Yen-Kuo 沈延國 , Chi Chang T'ai-yen hsien-sheng 記章太炎先生 (Taipei: Wen-hai ch'u-pan she, n.d.), pp. 51-52, 87-88.

[27]See NPCP, v. 2, pp. 958-959, 974-975; BDRC, v. 1, p. 96. Chih-yen was founded in September, 1935, and it published in total sixty-three issues. See also Shen, op. cit., p. 88.

a political party revived by T'ao Ch'eng-chang 陶成章 (1877-1911).[28] As president of the party, and chief editor of the journal, Chang claimed that the purpose of the journal was "to preserve the national heritage, promote learning and literature and benefit compulsory education."[29] Chang, in his advocation of the national heritage, published an article in the journal,[30] criticizing those who were biased against Chinese learning, stating "that they worshipped the learning of other countries without reservation and rejected indiscriminately Chinese learning no matter how good or bad it was."[31] Chang thus urged Chinese people not to reject the good points of either Chinese or foreign cultures. At the time Chang was also a frequent contributor to the scholarly journal, the Academic World (Hsüeh-lin 學林), edited by Chang's favorite disciple Huang K'an. The Academic World published only two issues in total. Chang wrote a number of scholarly essays for the journal, and his writings formed almost the entire content of these issues.[32] Chang was also engaged in an extensive revision of his famous book, Ch'iu-shu

---

[28]The journal was founded in Japan on March 10, 1910. See NPCP, v. 1, pp. 318-321; Mabel Lee, "Chang Ping-lin's Concept of Self and Society: Questions of Constancy and Continuity After the 1911 Revolution", p. 609.

[29]NPCP, v. 1, p. 322; Lee, op. cit., pp. 609-610.

[30]The article entitled "Chiao-yü te ken-pen yao ts'ung tzu-kuo tzu-hsin fa-ch'u-lai" 教育的根本要從自國自心發出來 was later collected in Chang T'ai-yen te pai-hua-wen, pp. 53-71.

[31]Ibid., p. 31; Lee, op. cit., p. 610.

[32]See Chiang, op. cit., p. 434; Wong, op. cit., p. 81.

訄書 (Book of Raillery) this year. It seems that Chang must have attached considerable importance to this book, for he published and revised Ch'iu-shu many times.[33] The first edition of Ch'iu-shu was completed in January, 1900, and published in February. The final edition was renamed and published in 1915 as Chien-lun 檢論 (the Re-examined Treatise).[34] The Ch'iu-shu was regarded as an important collection of Chang's political essays, and was published and revised during the years when Chang was most active in the political arena. However, many of the articles regarding the competing causes of reform or revolution were deleted, since, according to Chang himself, these writings were too shallow to be collected in this book. Instead, Chang collected and added many of his writings on the studies of the national heritage in the Ch'iu-shu or Chien-lun, for he believed they were worthy to be transmitted from generation to generation.[35]

Chang's concern to promote the Chinese national essence was also shown in his letter to Sun I-jang 孫詒讓(1848-1908), a prominent classical scholar in the late Ch'ing. In the letter, he told Sun that the national essence was apt to decay,

---

[33]T'ang Chih-chün, "Ts'ung Ch'iu-shu te hsiu-ting k'an Chang T'ai-yen te ssu-hsiang yen-pien" 從訄書的修訂看章太炎的思想演變 , Wen-wu 文物 , no. 11 (1975), pp. 59-74.

[34]See Chu Wei-cheng 朱維錚 , "Preface" to CTYCC, v. 3, pp. 1-20.

[35]Tang Chih-chün, "Ts'ung Ch'iu shu te hsiu-ting k'an Chang T'ai-yen te ssu-hsiang yen-pien", pp. 59-74; and NPCP, v. 1, pp. 314-315.

so he hoped that Sun would uphold the national essence and help to save it.[36] After the Wu-ch'ang Uprising in 1911, Chang even urged that Liu Shih-pei, while regarded as a traitor to the revolutionary camp and to the T'ung-meng hui, be forgiven and be allowed to promote Chinese culture.[37] Thus, apart from his involvement in politics, Chang devoted himself to the promotion of Chinese cultural heritage. This effort to preserve the national essence was the most consistent thread in his life.

The Origins of Chang's Concept of "National Essence"

The term kuo-ts'ui is a neologism borrowed from Japan, where the national essence movement emerged as a reaction against the wave of westernization in the Meiji period (1868-1912).[38] After Japan was forced by the Western Powers to end its seclusion policy in the mid-nineteenth century, it soon met the Western challenge by transforming itself into a new strong nation along Western lines. Although the change undergone by Meiji Japan saved it from national disaster, elements of the Japanese cultural heritage were sacrificed, and the people's

---

[36]NPCP, v. 1, pp. 246-247.

[37]Chang, "Hsüan-yen" 宣言 in CLHC, v. 2, p. 528.

[38]See Chang Hao, Chinese Intellectuals in Crisis, p. 118; Bernal, op. cit., p. 101.

cultural identity was shaken.[39]   Under the circumstances, a literary society,

Seikyosha　政教社　(Society for Political Education) was founded in 1888. Its

purpose was the preservation of Japan's "national essence" (kokusui hozon 國

粹保存).[40] Among its members, Miyake Setsurei　三宅雪嶺　(1860-1945) and

Shiga Shigetaka 志賀重昂 (1863-1927) were the most prominent. They claimed

that while they were committed to the adoption of Western institutions, it was more

important to preserve Japan's cultural tradition in order to maintain the basis for

cultural identity and national pride.[41]

While Shiga was devoted to the preservation of the national heritage, it

seemed that he was uncertain how to actually define kokusui. He refused to

include Shinto, Buddhism and Confucianism in his idea of kokusui. Therefore,

what he did was to define it as Japan's "artistic sense", which he contrasted with

the material West.[42] Although this definition later had an effect on the Chinese

national essence group,[43] it was not widely accepted by members of Seikyosha,

---

[39]See Kenneth B. Pyle, The New Generation in Meiji Japan: Problems of Cultural Identity, 1885-1895 (Stanford: Stanford University Press, 1969), pp. 1-5.

[40]Ibid., p. 5.

[41]Ibid.

[42]Ibid., pp. 67-68; Bernal, op. cit., p. 102.

[43]Bernal, op. cit., p. 102.

for it was not defined by appeal to Japanese tradition.[44] The Seikyosha finally
established a general definition, which had three attributes: (1) an intangible spirit,
(2) the special property of one country, and (3) a feature which could not be
copied by another country.[45]

The term kuo-ts'ui was introduced into China probably in the early 1900s by
overseas Chinese students in Japan. Chinese students began to study in Japan
in 1896, one year after China was defeated by Japan in the Sino-Japanese War.[46]
Chinese students were encouraged to study in Japan, for it was accessible and
provided important assets. For instance, Chang Chih-tung 張之洞 (1837-1909),
a prominent scholar-official, urged Chinese students to study in Japan, for the
Japanese had translated many materials from the West which were necessary for
Chinese people and had selected the essentials of Western learning in their
translations. Since the Japanese and Chinese languages were similar and the
former was thus easier than other languages for Chinese students to learn,
studying in Japan then had its advantage. He, therefore, noted that Chinese
students should study Western culture through Japan.[47] Terms translated into

---

[44]Pyle, op. cit., p. 69.

[45]Ibid., p. 70.

[46]See Marius Jansen, "Japan and the Chinese Revolution of 1911," in The
Cambridge History of China, v. 11, p. 348.

[47]Ibid., pp. 348-349.

Japanese also had some influence on the Chinese vocabulary. A recent study showed that over three-quarters of the new Chinese vocabulary of the late nineteenth century originated from Japanese.[48] The Japanese kuo-ts'ui entered the Chinese vocabulary as part of this massive infusion.

The Japanese neologism, kokusui, had several conceptual and terminological antecedents in Chinese thought. One was its linkage to the classical concept of t'i 體(substance) borrowed by nineteenth century reformers for special purposes. It was made famous by Chang Chih-tung as a slogan Chung-hsüeh wei t'i, Hsi-hsüeh wei yung 中學爲體，西學爲用(Chinese learning for the fundamental principles, Western learning for practical application), which Chang presented in his famous book, "Exhortation to Study" (Ch'üan-hsüeh p'ien 勸學篇) written in 1898.[49] However, Chang's slogan was primarily derived from the ideas of Feng Kuei-fen 馮桂芬 (1809-1874).[50] Feng, in his Chiao-pin-lu k'ang-i 校邠廬抗議 (Protests from the Chiao-pin Studio) written around 1860, had suggested, "If

---

[48]Ibid., p. 362.

[49]The slogan did not appear exactly the same as in the "Exhortation to Study," however, Chang did use the t'i-yung dualism in the book. See William Ayers, Chang Chih-tung and Educational Reform in China (Cambridge: Harvard University Press, 1971), pp. 150-151; Teng Ssu-yü, et al., China's Response to the West: A Documentary Survey, 1839-1923 (Cambridge: Harvard university Press, 1954). For Chang Chih-tung, see also ECCP, v. 1, pp. 27-32; Daniel H. Bays, China Enters the Twentieth Century: Chang Chih-tung and the Issues of a New Age, 1895-1909 (Ann Arbor: The University of Michigan Press, 1978).

[50]Teng Ssu-yü, China's Response to the West, pp. 50, 164.

Chinese moral principles and ethical teachings served as the original foundation, and were supplemented by the methods used by the various [Western] nations for the attainment of wealth and power, would this not be the best of all?"[51] Even before Chang Chih-tung formulated this slogan, some of his contemporaries, such as Tseng Kuo-fan 曾國藩 (1811-1872)[52] and Wang T'ao 王韜 (1828-1897)[53] had used this pair of terms.[54] In fact, the t'i-yung dichotomy had its origins among T'ang Buddhists and Sung Neo-Confucianists.[55]

Chang Chih-tung's usage was different from that of his classical predecessors. The concept had been primarily metaphysical, but Chang used the terms mainly in reference to politics and society. In the contexts of Buddhism and Neo-Confucianism, t'i and yung were inseparable; they were but two sides of the same coin. They implied each other. The t'i and yung of Chang Chih-tung, however, were separated into two different spheres. T'i referred to the Chinese "essence" and value; but yung was the material, practical western realm, Chang

---

[51]Ibid., p. 52. For Feng Kuei-fen, see ECCP, v. 1, pp. 241-243.

[52]For Tseng Kuo-fan, see ECCP, v. 2, PP. 751-756.

[53]For Wang T'ao, see ECCP, v. 2, pp. 836-839; Paul A. Cohen, Between Tradition and Modernity: Wang T'ao and Reform in Late Ch'ing China (Cambridge: Harvard University Press, 1974).

[54]See Wang Erh-min 王爾敏 , Wan-Ch'ing cheng-chih ssu-hsiang-shih lun 晚清政治思想史論 (Taipei: Hsüeh-sheng shu-chü, 1969), pp. 51-52, 56-57.

[55]Ayers, op. cit., p. 3.

sought to introduce to protect t'i.[56] His proposal drew criticism. Yen Fu 嚴復 (1853-1921) criticized Chang's misuse of the ancient idea of t'i and yung.[57] Yen noted that "Chinese learning has its t'i and yung; Western learning also has its t'i and yung."[58]

Yet the t'i-yung formula had its significance, for it was designed to uphold Chinese cultural heritage, and simultaneously to sanction the adoption of Western learning. After 1860, with the defeats and increasing humiliation in a number of foreign wars, a few scholars and officials were convinced of the need to adopt Western learning, which would save China from national disaster. However, they were still concerned about maintaining their own cultural heritage. But, the question was how to solve the dilemma -- to reconcile the conflict inherent in adopting Western learning while preserving the essentials of the Chinese tradition. In this circumstance, Chang Chih-tung's t'i-yung formula represented a conceptual, although probably impracticable, solution.[59]

---

[56]Ibid.

[57]See Wang Erh-min, op. cit., p. 52. Also see Fairbank et al. East Asia: The Modern Transformation (Boston: Houghton Mifflin, 1965), pp. 386-387. For criticisms of Chang Chih-tung's t'i-yung formula, see Joseph R. Levenson, Confucian China and its Modern Fate (Berkeley: University of California Press, 1965), v. 1, pp. 59-78. See also Ayers, op. cit., pp. 253-254.

[58]See quote in Wang Erh-min, op. cit., p. 52.

[59]Ayers, op. cit., pp. 1-4. See also Fairbank, East Asia: The Modern Transformation, p. 386.

Chang, in his "Exhortation of Study", also juxtaposed another pair of terms hsin-hsüeh 新學 (new learning) and chiu-hsüeh 舊學 (old learning),[60] and noted that "The old learning is for fundamental principles; the new learning is for practical application (chiu-hsüeh wei-t'i: hsin-hsüeh wei yung 舊學爲體，新學爲用)."[61] Apparently, the meanings of old learning and Chinese learning were the same, and so were the terms of new learning and Western learning. Western learning meant all kinds of knowledge imported from the West, that was quite different from China's traditional learning.[62] In the early 1900s, some Chinese intellectuals, such as Chang Ping-lin and Liu Shih-pei, used the concept of kuo-ts'ui to replace what Chang Chih-tung had described as t'i.[63] Thus, basically the original meaning of kuo-ts'ui was the same as that of Chung-hsüeh or chiu-hsüeh. One scholar concluded that the concept of kuo-ts'ui was primarily derived from the terms of Chung-hsüeh or chiu-hsüeh.[64]

---

[60]Ayers, op. cit., p. 151.

[61]See quote in Wang Erh-min, op. cit., pp. 54-55.

[62]See Hao Yen-p'ing and Wang Erh-min, "Changing Chinese Views of Western Relations, 1840-95 in The Cambridge History of China, v. 11, p. 169.

[63]See Guy S. Alitto, The Last Confucian: Liang Shu-ming and the Chinese Dilemma of Modernity (Berkeley: University of California Press, 1979), p. 6.

[64]See Ma Ying 馬瀛 , Kuo-hsüeh kai-lun 國學概論 (Taipei: Te-hua ch'u-pan she, 1978), pp. 2-3; Wang Tzu-ch'en 王淄塵 , Kuo-hsueh chiang-hua 國學講話 (Taipei: Hung-tao wen-hua shih-yeh yu-hsien kung-ssu, 1974), pp. 2-3.

Liang Ch'i-ch'ao probably was the first Chinese intellectual to mention the term, kuo-ts'ui. In 1902 Liang, in his letter to Huang Tsun-hsien 黃遵憲 (1848-1905), pointed out, "To nourish the people (kuo-min 國民), one should make it a principle to preserve the national essence, and should take old learning to polish and glorify it."[65] However, Liang abandoned usage of the term kuo-ts'ui after he had taken Huang Tsun-hsien's advice that what China really needed was not to promote national essence but to encourage the study of new learning.[66]

In 1903, when he was imprisoned in Shanghai, Chang Ping-lin started to promote the term kuo-ts'ui, which anticipated the founding of the Journal of National Essence in 1905.[67] While kuo-ts'ui was a Japanese neologism, Chang Ping-lin's k'ao-cheng studies established a broader conceptual base for his use of kuo-ts'ui than Chang Chih-tung had used. Now the term was associated with the idea of kuo-hsing 國性 (national character) from the readings of Ch'un-ch'iu in his early years.

---

[65]Ting Wen-chiang 丁文江 , Liang Jen-kung hsien-sheng nien-p'u ch'ang-pien ch'u-kao 梁任公先生年譜長編初稿 (Taipei: Shih-chieh shu-chü, 1962), v. 1, p. 161. See also Bernal, op. cit., p. 103.

[66]Bernal, op. cit., pp. 103-104.

[67]See Fan Ming-li 范明禮 , "Ch'ing-mo tzu-ch'an chieh-chi kuo-ts'ui-p'ai te chi-ke wen-t'i" 清末資產階級國粹派的幾個問題 in Hsin-hai ke-ming-shih ts'ung-k'an 辛亥革命史叢刊 (Peking: Hsin-hai ke-ming-shih pien-chi-tsu, 1987), v. 7, pp. 71-72.

An important idea in Ch'un-ch'iu was the distinction between Chinese and barbarians (Hua i chih pien 華夷之辨) which had inspired not only Chang's anti-Manchu sentiments during his childhood, but also his idea of kuo-hsing,[68] and he claimed that "the purpose of Confucius' Ch'un-ch'iu was to record people's conduct in order to preserve national character."[69] Since kuo-hsing was formed by historical and environmental forces, it was unique to each nation or race. He also asserted, "No matter how civilized or barbarous a nation is, its national character must be preserved."[70] The strength and survival of the nation, Chang argued, depended upon the preservation of its national character, just as he held that history also suggested that if a nation lost its kuo-hsing, its defeat and submission were inevitable.[71] He said, "After Russia defeated Poland, the Polish language was altered; the Turks destroyed the Eastern Roman Empire, and changed its customs; the Manchus occupied China, and destroyed its history."[72]

---

[68]See NPCP, v. 1, p. 6; and Chang's "Tao-han ch'ang-yen" 菿漢昌言 in CSTS, v. 2, p. 1118.

[69]See Chang's "Ching-hsüeh lüeh-shuo" 經學略說 in his Kuo-hsüeh lüeh-shuo 國學略說 (Hong Kong: Hong Kong huan-ch'iu wen-hua fu-wu-she, 1963), pp. 91-92; also see Yüan Nai-ying 袁乃瑛 , "Yü-hang Chang-shih chih ching-hsüeh" 餘杭章氏之經學 in Taiwan sheng-li shih-fan ta-hsueh kuo-wen yen-chiu-so chi-k'an 臺灣省立師範大學國文研究所集刊 no. 6 (June, 1962), p. 253.

[70]Chang Ping-lin, "Chiu hsüeh-pi lun" 救學弊論 in CTYCC, v. 5, p. 101.

[71]Ibid.

[72]Chang Ping-lin, "Ai fen-shu"哀焚書in CSTS, v. 1, p. 559; See also CTYCC, v. 3, p. 468.

The language, history and custom were included in the concept of Chang's <u>kuo-ts'ui</u>, and were necessary for the survival of a nation.[73] For Chang, the ideas of <u>kuo-ts'ui</u> and <u>kuo-hsing</u> were interchangeable, for both were unique features of a nation and their meanings were the same. Even in Japan, <u>kokusui</u> was identified as national character, and Shiga also translated <u>kokusui</u> as "nationality" or "national character".[74] However, probably attracted to the Japanese idea that the preservation of national essence could strengthen the nation, Chang Ping-lin adopted the phrase <u>kuo-ts'ui</u> and later on assumed the preservation of national essence as his life-long mission.

The Scope and Meaning of "National Essence" in Chang's Thought

Chang's speech in 1906 at the welcoming party held in Tokyo in his honor, partially spelled out his <u>kuo-ts'ui</u> idea publically. He claimed that there were three aspects of <u>kuo-ts'ui</u>: China's spoken and written languages (<u>yü-yen wen-tzu</u>語言文字), China's laws and institutions (<u>tien-chang chih-tu</u>　典章制度　) and accomplishments of great men in China's past (<u>jen-wu shih-chi</u>　人物事跡　). He also juxtaposed religion (<u>tsung-chiao</u> 宗教), or more precisely, Buddhism (<u>fo-chiao</u>　佛教　　), and <u>kuo-ts'ui</u> as two of the most important points of his

---

[73]<u>Ibid</u>.

[74]Pyle, <u>op. cit.</u> p. 67.

speech.[75]   In fact, Buddhism was an important element in his kuo-ts'ui

concept.[76] Chang continued to expand the content of kuo-ts'ui and in an article

he included customs (feng-su 風俗).[77] Thus, according to Chang himself, his

concept of kuo-ts'ui comprised of the aspects of China's spoken and written

languages, China's laws and institutions, accomplishments of great men in China's

past, China's customs and Buddhism.

The 1906 speech presented Chang's main ideas. First, he talked about the

aspect of China's spoken and written languages.   Chang said, "the Chinese

languages are unique.   Each word in Chinese has one immutable form.   Each

word has its own original meaning and derivative meanings."[78] However, they

were the same word which needed no change by means of derivative affixes as

that of foreign languages. Chang said, "For example, the word t'ien 天 , its

---

[75]See Chang's "Wo te p'ing-sheng yü pan-shih fang-fa", pp. 91-96.

[76]For example, Chang published lecture notes (chiang-i 講義) for the Society
for the Promotion of National Studies, which included the subject of Buddhism (nei-
tien hsüeh 內典學). Also, Chang's Seminar for National Studies included the
subject of Buddhism as well. Obviously in Chang's view, Buddhism was one of the
subjects under the category of his concept of kuo-hsüeh or kuo-ts'ui. See NPCP,
v. 1, pp. 215, 217; Also see Sung Chiao-jen, op. cit., p. 249.

[77]See Chang's "Ai fen-shu", in CTYCC, v. 3, pp. 323-324.

[78]See Chang's "Wo te p'ing-sheng", pp. 96-97.

original meaning is heaven. Its derived meanings are `esteemed' and then `nature'. These three meanings are different, but they are just one word t'ien."[79]

Chang noted the relationship between spoken and written Chinese. While China had hundreds of local dialects, so different from each other that they were mutually unintelligible, China has always had only one uniform written language. Thus, no matter how different spoken local dialects were, literate Chinese could communicate with each other through writing. The written language, thus, provided China an instrument of cultural unification.[80] With this in mind, Chang objected to the adoption of Esperanto as a language reform advocated by Wu Chih-hui 吳稚暉 (1864-1953), who was in favor of replacing the existing Chinese written language with an alphabetic writing system, or a system of romanization. If the Chinese written language was changed to Esperanto, Chang noted, China would undergo a drastic cultural upheaval and the change would have far-reaching effects on communication.[81] The adoption of the alphabetic system, Chang said, would also create difficulties for people in the study of ancient books. For through written languages, literate Chinese had access to ancient books for understanding

---

[79]Ibid., p. 97.

[80]See Chang's "Fang-yen" 方言 in CTYCC, v. 3, pp. 205-207; CSTS, v. 2, p. 836, and v. 1, p. 421.

[81]CSTS, v. 1, p. 421; See also Chiang, op. cit., p. 469; For Chang's refuting Wu's adoption of Esperanto see Chang's "Po Chung-kuo yung wan-kuo hsin-yu shuo" 駁中國用萬國新語說 in CSTS, v. 2, pp. 832-841.

China's past. For Chang, the written language was not just an element of a people's cultural heritage, but was also the source of the major distinction between human beings and animals. He said, "What separates people from the birds and beasts is that they have the idea of what is past . . . . . . If people have no idea of their past, what is the difference between them and the birds as well as the beasts?"[82]

Although Chang rejected the adoption of Esperanto, he advocated the unification of China's spoken language, for diverse local dialects made it difficult for people to communicate with each other. Chang also pointed out that it was necessary to create new words in order to meet the needs of modern times. However, these new words, he said, had to be created by philologists, for they would make these words properly according to the six major principles of Chinese writing (liu-shu 六書).[83]

The second aspect was China's laws and institutions. He began his comment this way:

> The particularly excellent institution in China is chün-t'ien 均田 (equal-field) system, which can not be matched by the West. It equals socialism not to mention the ching-t'ien 井田 (well-field) system, carried out during the Three Dynasties (2183-249 B.C.); even from Wei-Chin (220-420) to T'ang dynasties, the chün-t'ien system was put into practice, therefore, the gap between the rich and the poor

---

[82]CTYCC, v. 4, p. 366.

[83]See CTYCC, v. 3, pp. 209-210; Wong Young-tsu, op. cit., p. 65; Chang's "Wo te p'ing-sheng", pp. 97-98.

was not very great and the local governments could easily implement their policies.[84]

Chang's naive equation of the chün-t'ien system and "socialism" marked the recent Chinese interest in the Western tradition. Socialism was introduced into China probably after 1902 through Liang Ch'i-ch'ao. Liang founded the Kuang-chih shu-chü 廣智書局 (Extension of Knowledge Bookstore) in 1902,[85] and in the following year, three books on socialism were published by the bookstore. Although from 1903-1911 no further books on socialism were published, a number of articles on this subject did appear after 1903.[86] Socialism was in vogue among Chinese intellectuals, and many T'ung-meng hui members advocated socialism.[87]

It seemed that Chang easily gained information on socialism, while working at Liang's Bookstore in 1902.[88] Basically, Chang saw socialism as a doctrine which stressed the elimination of the existence of social and economic inequalities. As a classical scholar, Chang tended to find socialism in China's cultural heritage.

---

[84]Chang, "Wo te p'ing-sheng", p. 98.

[85]See Martin Bernal, Chinese Socialism to 1907 (Ithaca: Cornell University Press, 1976), pp. 90-91; and his "The Triumph of Anarchism over Marxism, 1906-1907" in Mary C. Wright, ed., China in Revolution: The First Phase, 1900-1913 (New Haven: Yale University Press, 1968), pp. 99-100.

[86]Bernal, "The Triumph of Anarchism", pp. 100-101.

[87]For example, Feng Tzu-yu (1881-1958), Sung Chiao-jen (1882-1913), Chu Chih-hsin 朱執信 (1885-1920), among others.

[88]NPCP, v. 1, p. 137. Chang translated a book entitled Sociology (She-hui-hsüeh 社會學) from Japanese for Liang's bookstore.

He thus linked socialism to all Chinese laws and institutions, including the chün-t'ien system. Chang pointed out, "All the other Chinese laws and institutions correspond to socialism, and even the very bad ones are still close to socialism."[89] He gave two examples: the legal system and the civil service examination system. Chang held, "The Chinese legal system was nearly cruel." However, it contained elements of socialism, for punishments were applied to all, no matter how rich or poor.[90] "The Civil Service Examination, originally an institution of very poor quality", according to Chang, was linked to socialism because it provided chances for everyone, especially the poor people, to become officials.[91] Thus, Chang concluded, "These two institutions initially were very bad ones, however, they still contained elements of socialism, not to say the other good ones."[92] In short, all of China's institutions tended toward socialism, because they could apply equally to all, and "today, when we worship Chinese laws and institutions we only revere our socialism." Therefore, he continued, "Although those bad ones should be reformed, those good ones should be revered."[93]

---

[89]Chang, "Wo te p'ing-sheng", p. 98.

[90]Ibid., pp. 98-99.

[91]Ibid., p. 99.

[92]Ibid.

[93]Ibid.

The third aspect was that of the accomplishments of great men in China's past. Chang first mentioned Liu Yü 劉裕 (356-422) and Yüeh Fei 岳飛 (1103-1141), who deserved to be admired greatly, for "they employed southern troops to defeat the barbarians, and [their examples] can heighten our spirit."[94] He continued to mention accomplishment by men of learning. Chang held, "The most learned men were philosophers in the Chou and Ch'in dynasties", and he also spoke highly of Chinese philosophy, for it could compete with European and Indian philosophies.[95] While Chang praised Confucianism in general, he rejected Sung-Ming Neo-Confucianism. He cited Tai Chen as a scholar who deserved esteem, for while his book did not openly attack the Manchus, it implied an anti-Manchu sentiment.[96] Thus, "if one intends to promote patriotic fervor, one has to take examples from all of these figures who have made great contributions to China's history."[97]

Chang's additions to this 1906 list were also important. Chang maintained that many of China's fine customs should be preserved to meet the needs of the nation, for China was not a newly founded nation. Chang then expressed his view

---

[94]Ibid., pp. 99-100.

[95]Ibid., p. 100

[96]Ibid. The book Chang mentioned here is Tai's Evidential Analysis of the Meanings of Terms in the Book of Mencius (Meng-tzu tzu-i shu-cheng 孟子字義 疏證), which was completed in 1777.

[97]Ibid.

on the fine customs which, he thought, should be retained, and on the improper

customs that should be prohibited:

(1) the marriage system should not be changed, however, early marriage

should be forbidden. To take a concubine should also be prohibited, for it

would undermine people's economy and conduct.

(2) the family system should be preserved.

(3) China initially did not establish a national religion, so no religion should

be founded as a national religion. However, religious beliefs should be on

the basis of free choice.

(4) gambling, horse racing and bull fights should be strictly prohibited, for

they would promote people's tendency to gain by luck and would interfere

with people's regular work.

(5) to imitate foreigners in dancing and kissing in public locations should be

banned by the police, because these would undermine public morality.[98]

Finally, was the aspect of Buddhism. Although Chang had studied some

Buddhist texts in the 1890s, he did not become a serious student of Buddhism

until he was imprisoned in Shanghai during the years 1903-1906 due to the Su-pao

case. Chang came to study Buddhism intensively at this time partly because in

---

[98]See Chang, "Chung-hua min-kuo lien-ho-hui ti-i-tz'u ta-hui yen-shuo-tz'u" 中華民國聯合會第一次大會演說詞 in CLHC, v. 2, pp. 534-535; see also Lee, op. cit., pp. 618-619. By "customs" Chang meant those established socially accepted practice in China.

86

prison Chang was only allowed to receive Buddhist books ,[99] and partly because during the imprisonment Chang was subjected to both physical and spiritual suffering and Buddhism provided him with spiritual refuge.[100] Another reason why Chang accepted Buddhism at this time was that he found that the approach of Buddhism and that of Han Learning were similar. As Chang said, "when I was imprisoned in Shanghai, I studied exclusively the works of Maitreya and Vasubandhu, whose approach is to start to analyze the concepts (ming-hsiang 名相) and to end by disproving these concepts. This approach resembled my life-long pursuit of sound learning or unadorned learning (p'u-hsüeh 樸學) and was, therefore, easy to accept."[101]

Upon his release from prison, Chang became a devotee of Buddhism and started to promote its doctrines. Chang asserted that Buddhism was the religion most suitable to China. For as he said, "Basically, China may be called a Buddhist country. Buddhist theory forces the most intelligent to believe in it, and its vinaya rules or rules of disicipline (chieh-lü 戒律) do the same to the imbecile."[102]

---

[99]Shen Yen-Kuo, op. cit., pp. 618-619.

[100]See Chang's "Tsou Jung chuan" 鄒容傳 in CTYCC, v. 4, p. 216; see also Chang Hao, Chinese Intellectuals in Crisis, p. 120.

[101]Chang, "Tao-han wei-yen" in CSTS, v. 2, p. 960. Translation adopted with minor change from Liang Ch'i-ch'ao, Intellectual Trends in the Ch'ing Period, p. 112.

[102]Chang, "Wo te p'ing-sheng", p. 93. See also Gasster, op. cit., p. 199.

Moreover, Buddhism was compatible with Confucianism in its fundamental spirit, that is, "Rely upon oneself, and not upon others (i-tzu bu i-t'a 依自不依他)."[103] The forms Buddhism he favored were Hua-yen 華嚴 (Flower Garland) School, Fa-hsiang 法相 (Dharma-Character) School and Ch'an or Zen 禪 (Meditation) School. However, he excluded Ching-t'u 淨土 (Pure Land) School, for Chang held that it contained elements of superstition.[104]

Chang regarded Buddhism highly because it could be used to promote people's morality for the cause of revolution.[105] And the promotion of morality was necessary for the survival of a nation. As Chang said, "The decay of morality is the fundamental reason for the fall of a nation and the race."[106] He continued, "People without morality cannot devote themselves to revolution."[107] In Buddhism, Chang did find elements that would be most useful in promoting people's morality. For instance, the emphasis on self-reliance in the Ch'an, Hua-yen and Fa-hsiang Schools, and the idea of the Fa-hsiang School that all

---

[103]Chang, "Ta T'ieh-cheng" 答鐵錚 in CTYCC, v. 4, p. 369. T'ieh-cheng is the pen name of Lei Chao-hsing 雷照性 . See also Chang, "Wo te p'ing-sheng", p. 94; Chan Sin-wai, op. cit., p. 149.

[104]Chang, "Wo te p'ing-sheng", p. 93.

[105]Ibid., p. 95-96.

[106]Chang, "Ke-ming tao-te shuo" 革命道德說 in CTYCC, v. 4, p. 277.

[107]Ibid., p. 279; see also Gasster, op. cit., pp. 206-207.

phenomena are illusory would foster people's will to abandon even their lives for the cause of revolution.[108]

Although Confucianism also stressed the teaching of morality, Chang did not introduce it for promoting revolutionary morality. For while Confucianism had some good features, it also contained some elements linked with the pursuit of wealth and high position, that would fail to benefit the revolutionary movement.[109]

Chang's commitment to Buddhism also led him to criticize the doctrines of Christianity bitterly. For instance, he rejected the idea of Christianity that Jehovah or God was transcendental, omniscient and omnipotent, absolute, and all-encompassing.[110] Chang pointed out that although Christianity had helped make what the West it is today, it still was an inferior religion for its doctrines were even mutually contradictory and clashed with philosophy in general, and therefore were unsuitable for China.[111] Like most of his contemporaries, Chang rejected Christianity due to its affiliation with Western imperialism, and its contradiction to Chinese indigenous thoughts.[112]

---

[108]Chang, "Wo te p'ing-sheng", pp. 93-94; Chan Sin-wai, op. cit., pp. 45-46.

[109]Chang, "Wo te p'ing-sheng", pp. 91-92.

[110]Chang, "Wu-shen lun" 無神論 , in CTYCC, v. 4, pp. 396-398; Chan Sin-wai, op. cit., p. 45.

[111]Chang, "Wo te p'ing-sheng", pp. 91-93.

[112]See Chan Sin-wai, op. cit., p. 157.

While Chang was an advocate of Mahayana Buddhism, he did not attempt to establish a "Buddhist World View,"[113] for Buddhism was perceived by Chang as a means to elevate morality, which, in turn, was necessary for achieving the revolutionary ends. Since in Chang's eyes Buddhism was a means, not an end, Chang even claimed, "The day when the morality prevails is the day the religion [or more precisely, Buddhism] will disappear."[114] More important was that Buddhism was an important element of Chang's kuo-ts'ui idea that Chang formulated to counteract the intrusion of Western culture, the purpose of which was to protect China's national pride and its cultural identity. Chang maintained that China's cultural identity and its pride arose directly from its own cultural heritage.

Chang's advocacy of the preservation of the national essence was at first seen as an angst for China's cultural identity, threatened by the Western impact.[115] As he said, "People are ashamed that our culture is different from that of the West, however, I am rather proud that they are different."[116] For Chang, China's culture was its special property. As he said, "Chinese history is

---

[113]This view is held by Chang Hao in his <u>Chinese Intellectuals in Crisis</u>.

[114]Chang, "Chien-li tsung-chiao lun" 建立宗教論 in <u>CTYCC</u>, v. 4, p. 418; see also Wong Young-tsu, <u>op</u>. <u>cit</u>., p. 55.

[115]See Chang Hao, <u>Chinese Intellectuals in Crisis</u>, p. 118.

[116]Chang, "Yüan hsüeh" 原學 , in <u>CTYCC</u>, v. 1, p. 478. See also Chang Hao, <u>Chinese Intellectuals in Crisis</u>, p. 119.

absolutely a history of Han Chinese, which can not be universalized by any other culture."[117] He continued, "Both Chinese philology and history are China's unique learning, not universal learning."[118] For Chang the culture of each nation was formed by its own historical experience. Therefore, national identity must come from its own cultural uniqueness. Without it, China could not maintain its national identity. More than that, as a classical scholar, Chang was very aware that the preservation of the national essence was essential for the survival of the nation.

Chang's conception of the national essence was also influenced by his reaction to intellectual trends, as shown in his criticism of K'ang Yu-wei's interpretation of Chinese culture. Chang observed that K'ang's interpretation of Chinese classics was the distortion of Chinese history for his political purpose. For instance, Chang repudiated K'ang's use of Confucius as a political weapon in portraying Confucius as a uncrowned sage-king or even a prophet who had set up a model for institutional change throughout history into a future Golden Age. Chang's rejection was simple: how could Confucius anticipate the problems of

---

[117]See quote in Wong Young-tsu, "K'ang Yu-wei Chang Ping-lin ho-lun" 康有爲，章炳麟合論 in Chung-yang yen-chiu-yüan chin-tai shih yen-chiu-so chi-k'an 中央研究院近代史研究所集刊 (Taipei: Chung-yang yen-chiu-yüan chin-tai-shih yen-chiu-so, June, 1986), v. 15, pt. 1, p. 135.

[118]See quote in NPCP, v. 1, p. 295.

modern times?[119] By the same token, Chang also rejected K'ang's assertion that Confucius held an revolutionary view of China's history, conforming to a three stages model -- from the age of decay and chaos to the age of universal peace -- and following a unilinear, irreversible process of development.[120] Chang thought that this did not represent an objective study of history but only a way to use the image of history to predict the future.[121] Being uncomfortable with K'ang's arbitrary interpretations of China's history, Chang came to re-examine and to re-evaluate Chinese cultural heritage, from which Chang found some elements were essential and some were not. This process stimulated Chang's formulation of his concept of kuo-ts'ui.

The scope of the national essence ideas might seem to make it a kind of wholesale, indiscriminate affirmation of China's cultural heritage.[122] However, this was not the case, for Chang viewed Chinese culture in a very critical way and was quite definite about which elements were to be maintained. This was evident in his evaluation of Confucianism and Buddhism. Although he regarded

---

[119]See Wang Fan-sen, op. cit., p. 56. For K'ang Yu-wei see Hsiao Kung-chuan, A Modern China and a New World: K'ang Yu-wei, Reformer and Utopian, 1858-1927 (Seattle: University of Washington Press, 1975).

[120]See Chang Hao, Chinese Intellectuals in Crisis, pp. 50-55.

[121]Chang, "Cheng-hsin lun" 徵信論 in CTYCC, v. 4, p. 59. See also Wang, op. cit., p. 53.

[122]See Chang Hao, Chinese Intellectuals in Crisis, p. 119.

Confucianism and Buddhism highly, he did not consider all their elements as essentials to be included in the kuo-ts'ui idea. For instance, Chang excluded Confucian ideas linked with self-interest.[123] He also excluded the Ching-t'u School of Mahayana Buddhism, for it seemed to emphasize superstition.[124] Another example was Chang's critical perceptions of Confucius. Although Chang regarded "Confucius as a great historian", because of his efforts to eliminate superstition, gods and spirits from Chinese culture, he also portrayed Confucius as an unprincipled scholar.[125] Chang's acceptance of the cultural past entailed selectivity; that legacy to be preserved -- the national essence -- meant those historical and cultural attributes of China which were appropriate to a modern nation.

---

[123]Chang, "Wo te p'ing-sheng", p. 92.

[124]Ibid.

[125]See Chang, "Chu-tsu-hsüeh lüeh-shuo"　諸子學略說　in CLHC, v. 1, pp. 288-291 and "Ting-K'ung"　訂孔　in CTYCC, v. 3, p. 135.

CHAPTER 4

CHANG'S PATH TO REVOLUTION

While Chang Ping-lin was still a student at the <u>Ku-ching</u> Academy, he became involved in the reform movement which began after 1894. In 1895 Chang became an active reformist, and after 1900, a prominent revolutionary. Inasmuch as he was a serious student of the School of Han Learning, which stressed scholarship as purely textual studies divorced from politics, Chang found himself in a dilemma between scholarship and politics; which should be his priority, the promotion of national cultural heritage or national survival? How did Chang resolve this contradiction?

Although Chang's anti-Manchu sentiments began during his childhood, he became a reformist before he became a revolutionary. Why did he favor reform when he was first involved in politics? Chang was also regarded as a racist, or an "ethnocentric nationalist",[1] for he was prominent as an anti-Manchu revolutionary who had drawn a distinct line between the Manchus and the Han Chinese race. However, was it really the case?

During his life, Chang had at different times been a supporter of reform and at other times a supporter of revolution. He was a revolutionary who called for the

---

[1]See Charlotte Furth, "The Sage as Rebel: The Inner World of Chang Ping-lin" in <u>The Limits of Change</u>, pp. 117, 138, 149.

preservation of China's national essence.[2] He was known as a great classical scholar and yet he criticized Confucianism.[3] Furthermore, he advocated republicanism and yet condemned representative government.[4] The result of this has been a view that his ideas, taken together, seemed to be contradictory.[5] However, was it as real as scholars suggested? This chapter will examine these and related questions under two headings: first, Chang as a reformist and second, Chang as a revolutionist.

Chang as a Reformist

After China was defeated in the Sino-Japanese War of 1894-1895, many Chinese intellectuals became convinced that it was imperative for China to undertake far-reaching reforms to survive as an independent nation. This defeat had greater impact on the Chinese than any of the other defeats China had previously suffered by foreign powers.[6] With this war the efforts of self-strengthening reforms which has been under way for more than two decades failed

---

[2]See Chang, "Wo te p'ing-sheng", pp. 91-101.

[3]Ibid., pp. 91-92.

[4]Chang, "Tai-i jan-fou lun" 代議然否論 in Chou Hung-jan, ed., Chang T'ai-yen hsüan-chi 章太炎選集 (Taipei: P'a-mi-erh shu-tien, 1979), pp. 123-134.

[5]See Gasster, op. cit., p. 221.

[6]See Chang Hao, "Intellectual Change and the Reform Movement, 1890-8", p. 291.

as China's recently built modern navy was totally annihilated?[7] It seemed particularly shocking to most Chinese that China could be defeated even by a very small country which most Chinese had regarded as far inferior to China in both culture and power.[8] This defeat thus awakened most Chinese from the dream that by the adoption of Western technology in the form of self-strengthening China could become a great power.[9] Therefore, many Chinese intellectuals began to realize that unless China implemented fundamental changes in the government, the survival of the nation would come into question. K'ang Yu-wei's reformism became prominent in this intellectual ferment.

K'ang had petitioned the throne for the need of reform in 1888[10] to no avail . And only in 1895 after China's defeat did any large scale reform begin.[11] In this year, when K'ang was in Peking for the metropolitan civil service examination, he rallied hundreds of his fellow examination candidates to petition for resistance against the Japanese invasion and for initiating reform.[12] In

---

[7]See Hsü, "Late Ch'ing Foreign Relations, 1866-1905" in The Cambridge History of China, v. 11, pp. 106-107.

[8]Chang Hao, "Intellectual Change and the Reform Movement, 1890-8", p. 291.

[9]See Leung Man-kam, "Chang Ping-lin: His Life and Career", Lien-ho shu-yüan hsüeh-pao 聯合書院學報   , no. 8 (1970), p. 97.

[10]Chang Hao, "Intellectual Change and the Reform Movement, 1890-8", p. 291.

[11]Ibid.

[12]Ibid., pp. 291-292.

August, 1895, K'ang established the Society for the Study of Self-strengthening (Ch'iang-hsüeh hui 強學會) in Peking, aiming at political reform.[13] Two months later, a Shanghai branch was also founded by K'ang.[14]

While Chang was still studying at the Ku-ching Academy, he learned of the humiliating defeat of China by Japan in 1894: it stimulated Chang's involvement in politics. He observed that the state of the nation was deplorable, and it was an age in which some wise men even became recluses.[15] As he said, "When China was faced with partition [by foreign powers], I could not bear it."[16] Thus, like many intellectuals of the time, Chang was roused to action. In 1895, Chang sent a contribution and enlisted in K'ang's Ch'iang-hsüeh hui in Shanghai.[17] The next year Chang left Ku-ching Academy when he was invited to join the editorial staff of the reformist journal Shih-wu pao 時務報 (Current Affairs Journal), edited by Liang Ch'i-ch'ao.[18]

---

[13]Ibid., p. 293.

[14]Ibid., p. 294.

[15]See Chang, "Ming-tu" 明獨 in Chiang I-hua and Chu Wei-cheng 朱維錚 , eds., Chang T'ai-yen hsüan-chi 章太炎選集 (Shanghai: Jen-min ch'u-pan she, 1981), p. 8; also see Lee, "Chang Ping-lin's Concept of Self and Society", p. 601.

[16]Chang, "Ming-tu", p. 7.

[17]TTNP, p. 5.

[18]Ibid.

Chang's departure from the academy was disapproved by his teacher, Yü Yüeh, who regarded it as a betrayal of the tradition of the School of Han Learning, which stressed the study for the sake of study with no political involvement. Chang's involvement in politics did place him in a dilemma of choice between scholarship and politics.[19] However, Chang's conviction that the preservation of national culture could save the nation appeared to provide a resolution to this contradiction. Thus, while Chang was involved in politics, he never gave up the evidential scholarship of the school, for Chang believed that the survival of the nation depended on the survival of the national culture, and that the preservation of the national culture could strengthen the nation. Obviously, politics was perceived by Chang only as a means to protect China's culture. Even after Chang had become a revolutionary, he paid a visit to Yü Yüeh in 1901, who still scolded him very bitterly for his engagement in radical politics. Chang defended himself by appealing to the example of Ku Yen-wu, the founder of Han Learning, who combined scholarship with politics to justify his political involvement or anti-Manchuism.[20] Chang said, "The purpose of Ku's devotion to ching-hsüeh 經學 (classical studies) was to trace the origin of kuo-hsing 國性 (national character) and to draw a distinction between Han Chinese and barbarians [the Manchus]."[21]

---

[19]Chang Hao, Chinese Intellectuals in Crisis, p. 105.

[20]TTNP, p. 8; see also Chang Hao, Chinese Intellectuals in Crisis, pp. 105-106.

[21]TTNP, p. 8.

Thus, Chang's devotion to political radicalism was largely as a means to protect China's cultural heritage and to guarantee its continuity especially when China's culture was threatened with extinction by foreign powers.

While Chang had been exposed to anti-Manchu ideas in his early years, he did not become an instant revolutionary. In fact, he supported K'ang-Liang's reform from 1895. Chang was in favor of reform rather than revolution, because at that time K'ang-Liang's initiative was the most influential among those advocating change.[22] Besides, Chang at that time did not approve of Sun Yat-sen's activities of revolution, for he doubted if Sun's revolution would benefit China. More important as far as Chang was concerned was that one of K'ang's reform aims was protect Chinese culture from the Western challenge; this shared goal permitted Chang to support K'ang in the mid-1890s. Although reform and revolution were regarded as the most practical means to deal with China's political crisis, until 1905-09 most people were attracted to join the camp of reform, for they believed that reform would offer the greatest hopes to resolve China's problems.[23]

Although Sun Yat-sen had advocated revolution in 1894,[24] it seemed that

---

[22]Lee, op. cit., p. 602.

[23]Ibid., p. 598.

[24]Gasster, op. cit., pp. 28-29; for the study of Sun Yat-sen, see Harold Z. Schiffrin, Sun Yat-sen and the Origins of the Chinese Revolution (Berkeley: University of California Press, 1968).

Chang was not attracted by Sun's political activities, for Chang did not think Sun's revolutionary activities would be promising, and he, before meeting Sun, even dismissed him as an "uncultured outlaw".[25] Sun Yat-sen had founded the revolutionary organization, the Hsing-Chung hui 興中會 (Society to Revive China), in Honolulu in 1894, however, it had only a few members.[26] He also launched an uprising in Canton in 1895. The Chinese revolution was thus under way. However, the revolt was quickly suppressed by the Manchu government.[27] Even after his work on revolution for nine years, it had borne little fruit. By 1903, his revolutionary camp gained only little support and was short of funds, members and military equipment.[28] Thus, by 1903, no one would regard Sun as a promising revolutionary.

Besides, Sun was perceived by his own contemporaries, especially the intellectuals, as a bandit (k'ou 寇). For example, Wu Ching-heng 吳敬恒 (1864-1953) despised Sun as a "rustic ruffian", and even suspected that he was illiterate in Chinese.[29] This image was probably because Sun had received

---

[25]See Chang, "Ch'in Li-shan chuan" 秦力山傳 , in CTYCC, v. 5, p. 185; see also Hsüeh Chün-tu, Huang Hsing and the Chinese Revolution (Stanford: Stanford University Press, 1961), p. 33.

[26]Gasster, op. cit., p. 28.

[27]Ibid., p. 29.

[28]Ibid., p. 30.

[29]See Schiffrin, op. cit., p. 300.

Western education overseas in his early years. Chang also indicated that the students in Japan thought that Sun was hard to get along with and they were rather indifferent toward him.[30] However, the suspicion was probably mutual, for Sun was also skeptical of trusting the intellectuals and students in the revolutionary movement.[31] This was evident in that Sun did not attempt to recruit the intellectuals and students into Hsing-Chung hui, and he gained the support mostly from overseas Chinese.[32] While Chang was appreciative of Sun's anti-Manchu cause, he did not support revolution, not only because Chang suspected Sun's personality and leadership at that time, but because he doubted that revolution would save China.

Chang had first begun to take notice of Sun in 1896, when Sun was kidnapped in the Chinese embassy in London. Chang asked Liang Ch'i-ch'ao who Sun was? Liang told him that Sun was a die-hard anti-Manchu advocator. Chang was very much impressed.[33] While Chang was impressed with Sun who had dared to advocate anti-Manchu revolution, he perceived Sun as "a man who was

---

[30]Hsüeh, op. cit., p. 35.

[31]Schiffrin, op. cit., p. 300.

[32]See Chang Yü-fa 張玉法 , Ch'ing-chi te ke-ming t'uan-t'i 清季的革命團體 (Taipei: Chung-yang yen-chiu-yüan chin-tai-shih yen-chiu-so, 1982), p. 202.

[33]See Chu Hsi-tsu 朱希祖 , "Pen-shih Chang T'ai-yen hsien-sheng k'ou-shou shao-nien shih-chi pi-chi" 本師章太炎先生口授少年事蹟筆記 , Chih-yen), v. 35 (1936), p. 1; see also Leung, op. cit., p. 102.

unstable and not trustworthy, and thus, he could not become a Chang Chiao

張角(?-184) or Wang Hsien-chih 王仙芝 (?-878)."[34] Chang also thought that

revolution would bring chaos and lead to the division of China by the foreign

powers, and only reform could save China. Thus, even though Sun had

formulated the main goal of the Hsing-Chung hui as the overthrow of the

Manchus,[35] Chang did not join in Sun's revolutionary camp. In any case,

Chang's anti-Manchu sentiments at that time could take no more radical form than

refusal to take the Ch'ing civil service examinations.[36]

Chang supported K'ang's reform, because he shared K'ang's concern to

preserve China's tradition. At the very beginning, when K'ang proposed his

reform, he saw China was threatened by Western aggression both politically and

culturally. Apart from the national crisis, China also encountered a cultural crisis

threatened by the Western culture, especially Christianity. In order to meet the

Western challenge, it was therefore as important to preserve Chinese tradition or

teachings (pao-chiao 保教) as to preserve the nation (pao-kuo 保國). These

---

[34]See NPCP, v. 1, p. 83; see also Lee, op. cit., p. 612. Chang Chiao was a leader of the Yellow Turban Uprising at the close of the Eastern Han dynasty. He started a rebellion in 184 A.D. Wang Hsien-chih was a leader of the peasant rebellion in the Late T'ang. He began his uprising in 875 A.D.

[35]Gasster, op. cit., p. 30.

[36]NPCP, v. 1, p. 7; see also Rankin, op. cit., p. 54.

two goals thus formed the core of K'ang's reform program.[37] The objectives of K'ang's reform movement were formulated in the "Set of Regulations" (chang-ch'eng 章程) of the Pao-kuo hui 保國會 (Society to Protect the Nation), which was formed in the spring of 1898. The aim of the society as stated in Article 2, was "to preserve intact the country's territory, its people, and its tradition" (pao-ch'uan kuo-t'u, kuo-min, kuo-chiao 保全國土、國民、國教), or as defined in Article 9, "to study matters relative to the preservation of the country, the race and the tradition." (chiang-ch'iu pao-kuo, pao-chung, pao-chiao chih shih 講求保國、保種、保教之事).[38]

While he was a supporter of the reform, Chang was said to have already objected to K'ang's interpretation of Confucianism due to their doctrinal differences.[39] Since K'ang was an advocate of the New Text School, and Chang was said to be an adherent of the Ancient Text School, scholars suggested that the conflict between these two scholars was a revival of the dispute between the New Text and Ancient Text Schools.[40] However, it was not necessarily the case. As we have stated above, Chang's intellectual tendency was characterized by the

---

[37]See Chang Hao, "Intellectual Change and the Reform Movement, 1890-8", p. 285.

[38]Hsiao, op. cit., p. 104.

[39]NPCP, v. 1, p. 34.

[40]For example, see Kuo Chan-p'o 郭湛波 , Chung-kuo chin-tai ssu-hsiang-shih 中國近代思想史 (Hong Kong: Lung-men shu-tien, 1965), p. 267.

accommodation within the Han Learning of both the Ancient Text and the New Text persuasions. This undoubtedly was influenced by his teacher, Yü Yüeh, whose teaching included the scholarships of both of these schools. This was evident that Chang also adopted ideas from the New Text school in his own writings, when he was studying in the Ku-ching Academy. Even after Chang became a supporter of reform, he still continued to employ New Text concepts to promote the cause of reform. Therefore, Chang's refutation of K'ang's views was not the revival of the debate between the Ancient Text and the New Text Schools as scholars suggested.

Nevertheless, Chang did oppose K'ang's claim of the establishment of Confucianism as a state religion, for it made Chang feel uncomfortable.[41] For example, in 1896 when Chang joined the staff of Shih-wu pao, he asked Liang Ch'i-ch'ao what objectives K'ang was preaching. Liang answered that it was reform and the establishment of Confucianism as a state religion. Chang disapproved the latter by saying:

> Reform is the pressing and urgent matter to be dealt with today, however, to worship Confucius and to establish Confucianism as the state religion may risk the danger of stirring up religious agitation.[42]

---

[41]TTNP, p. 5.

[42]See Li Chien-nung 李劍農 , Tsui-chin san-shih nien Chung-kuo cheng-chih shih 最近三十年中國政治史 (Taipei: Hsueh-sheng shu-chu 1976), p. 112; see also Leung, op. cit , p. 100.

Chang's anti-religious commitment could also be seen in his reply to Liang Ting-fen

梁鼎芬 (dates unknown), on the staff of Chang Chih-tung. When Chang was asked

by Liang if K'ang intended to become emperor, Chang replied:

> I have only heard that K'ang attempts to become founder of a religion
> (chiao-chu 教主), but I have never heard that he wants to make himself
> emperor. In fact, it is nothing strange that one has the desire to become
> emperor, however, it is improper if one attempts to become founder of a
> religion.[43]

Chang's opposition to K'ang's Confucian religion was because of his

rational thinking as evidenced in his evaluation of Confucius. Chang regarded that

the greatness of Confucius lay in his ability to free Chinese culture from

superstitions, gods and spirits. Therefore, Chang asserted that the establishment

of Confucianism as a state religion as K'ang claimed was in effect to demote

Confucius' teachings, for it introduced elements of mysticism into Confucianism

that would make rational inquiry impossible.[44] Nevertheless, Chang's opposition

to K'ang's Confucian religion did not prevent him from supporting reform. Their

shared concern to preserve China's tradition in general was sufficient to override

their differences and permitted Chang to support K'ang's reform in the 1890s. It

was not until the 1900s that Chang started to purify his conceptions of the

elements of Chinese culture and to establish his own concept of China's national

essence; his different conception of tradition finally led him to counter K'ang's view

---

[43]See Feng, op. cit., v. 1, p. 95.

[44]See Wong, op. cit., p. 9.

on the interpretation of Confucianism, especially after their political differences were added.

In any case, Chang started his career as a reformist after 1895. After the collapse of the reform movement in 1898, Chang did allude to anti-Manchuism and even revolution. Nevertheless, Chang did not become openly a revolutionary until 1900, when he realized that the Manchu government was unable to resist the foreign powers in the Boxer Uprising.

In January, 1897, Chang left Ku-ching Academy for Shanghai to start his new position as the editorial staff of Shih-wu pao and to participate in political activities as a reformer. However, three months later Chang resigned because he had serious quarrels with many of K'ang's followers who supported K'ang's claim that Confucianism was a religion with which Chang felt uncomfortable.[45] However, Chang's resignation did not end his career as a reformer. Chang then returned to Hang-chou where he and Sung Shu organized Hsing-Che hui 興浙 會 (The Association for Reviving Chekiang).[46] Chang wrote a preface for the association that praised five heros in Chekiang history who bravely fought against the barbarians.[47] In the chang-ch'eng 章程 (Set of Regulations), they also

---

[45]See Chiang, op. cit., pp. 48-49.

[46]Ibid., pp. 49-50.

[47]Ibid., p. 51.

stressed the study of Chinese institutions and history.[48] In August, 1897, Chang

and Sung also founded <u>Ching-shih pao</u>　經世報　(The Statecraft Journal) with

Chang as its editor-in-chief. The aim of the journal was to advocate reform by

introducing new knowledge and theories from abroad.[49]

Chang also published a series of articles in the reformist journal, <u>Shih-hsüeh</u>

<u>pao</u>實學報(Journal of Practical Learning). These writings focused on a reappraisal

of the Confucian tradition and the noncannonical philosophies of pre-Ch'in times,

including Mohism, Taoism and Legalism. Chang maintained that Confucianism

and noncannonical philosophies could complement each other and Confucianism

thus should not monopolize Chinese cultural tradition,[50] for he saw that while

Confucianism had contributed significantly to the Chinese cultural heritage, it could

not be identified with Chinese culture because there were still other schools of

philosophies, such as Taoism and Mohism, in Chinese tradition. Thus, Chang

wrote these essays to call for a critical and unbiased attitude towards Chinese

culture. As for Confucianism, Chang was especially attracted by Hsün Tzu.[51]

Chang's fervent interest in Hsün Tzu owed largely to his discipline in Han Learning,

for the study of Hsün Tzu had been an undercurrent in the School of Han Learning

---

[48]<u>Ibid</u>., p. 52.

[49]<u>Ibid</u>., p. 53.

[50]<u>Ibid</u>., pp. 56-57.

[51]<u>TTNP</u>, p. 6.

since the mid-eighteenth century.[52] In an article entitled hou-sheng 後聖 (The Later Sage) published in the Shih-hsüeh pao, Chang even promoted Hsün Tzu's standing second only to Confucius in the Confucian tradition. Chang said that Hsün Tzu was a figure who was eligible to be regarded as the later Sage following Confucius.[53] For Chang asserted that like "Confucius who was superior to such ancient sages as Yao, Shun and Duke of Chou because he was able to have a clear break from gods and spirits in ancient times", Hsün Tzu also revealed "humanity and affairs" (jen-shih 人事) and was free from gods and spirits in his thinking.[54] According to Chang, before Han times Confucianism remained secular, it was only after the Han dynasty that some elements of the supernatural permeated Confucianism.[55] Following Hsün Tzu, Chang perceived Confucianism as a secular teaching which also revealed his rational thinking. Therefore, Chang's objective attitudes toward Chinese learning and his rational thinking provided him a basis to enable him not only to reappraise Chinese tradition but also to purify elements of Chinese cultural heritage and then to form his own conception of national essence afterwards.

In the spring of 1898, Chang left for Wu-ch'ang where he helped edit

---

[52]See Chang Hao, Chinese Intellectuals in Crisis, p. 107.

[53]NPCP, v. 1, p. 51.

[54]Ibid.; see also T'ang, CLHC, v. 1, p. 120.

[55]See Wong, op. cit., p. 17.

Cheng-hsüeh pao 正學報 (the Journal of Orthodox Learning) proposed by Chang Chih-tung, who was regarded by his contemporaries as an open-minded and progressive scholar-official.[56] However, Chang was soon dismissed, for he had quite different ideas for reform from Chang Chih-tung's. While Chang Chih-tung showed his loyalty to the monarchy, Chang Ping-lin's support of reform was not to protect the Manchu regime, but to save the nation.[57] One account also showed that Chang's dismissal was because Chang Chih-tung discovered that Chang Ping-lin's intention was improper and that some of his expressions humiliated the emperor and offended superiors.[58]

On June 11, 1898, the Kuang-hsü Emperor issued an edict to announce reform. However, the reform movement failed when the empress dowager launched a successful coup d'etat on September 21st. With the failure of the reform movement, Chang was driven into exile due to his former connections with the Shih-wu pao.[59] Chang then fled to Taiwan in December, 1898, where he obtained a position as a writer (chuan-shu 撰述) at the Taiwan Daily News (Taiwan jih-jih hsin-pao 臺灣日日新報).[60] After the collapse of the reform

---

[56]NPCP, v. 1, p. 63.

[57]Ibid., pp. 63-64.

[58]See Feng, op. cit., v. 1, p. 113.

[59]BDRC, v. 1, p. 93; se also Wong, op. cit., p. 13.

[60]Chiang, op. cit., p. 80.

movement in 1898, Chang, as an exile in Taiwan, did allude to anti-Manchuism. In an article, "Cheng-chiang lun" 正疆論 (On the Rectification of Territory), published in the Daily News, Chang said that "The Han Chinese hatred for the Manchus was not only because it was a different race" but because of its brutal conquest of China. Since the Han Chinese hated the Manchus so bitterly, "they could not live under the same sky."[61] Chang was also said to have written to K'ang and Liang, urging them not to be loyal to the Manchu dynasty. He said,

> Sun Wen [Sun Yat-sen] knows only a little about "foreign affairs" (yang-wu 洋務), however, he is still able to make distinction between the Han Chinese and the Manchus, and calls for revolution. Both of you are literati, but you fail to tell right from wrong, and are willing to serve the Manchu court. I am really regretful of that.[62]

While Chang was exposed to anti-Manchu ideas, he was also afraid that "if the Manchus were expelled at the time, the Western powers would take this occasion to seize China's territory."[63] Chang was thus in a dilemma as to whether to turn against the Manchus or not. To resolve this problem Chang made an expedient plan. He said that in order to meet the challenge of the West, the Kuang-hsü emperor could be accepted as the "guest ruler" (k'o-ti 客帝) or a feudal lord, and the descendant of Confucius should be honored as the ruler of China.[64] After

---

[61]Ibid., p. 86.

[62]See Feng, op. cit., v. 1, p. 113.

[63]Chang, "K'o-ti" in CTYCC, v. 3, p. 67.

[64]Ibid., pp. 65-69.

he stayed in Taiwan for about six months Chang made his first visit to Japan on June 14, 1899, where he first met Sun Yat-sen. They did not know each other very well at this time.[65] In any case, Chang remained a reformer in the 1890s. However, it should be remembered that Chang's support of reform was not to protect the Manchu regime, but to save the nation.

Chang as a Revolutionist

When Chang was a supporter of reform, he asserted that a successful reform would strengthen the ability of the Manchu government to resist foreign powers. His primary commitment to China meant that when the Manchu government failed to defend the nation against the foreign invasion in the Boxer Uprising in 1900, Chang would abandon the Manchus and become openly a revolutionary.[66] The choice of reform or revolution for Chang rested on assessments of means to save the nation; therefore, if reform could not save China, the only alterative could be revolution.

The event that prompted Chang to change his position was the Boxer Uprising in 1900. From the first allied actions of June sixteenth until the conclusion

---

[65]TTNP, p. 7.

[66]See Wong op. cit., p. 24.

of the Boxer protocol, 1901, China was clearly the victim of a national crisis.[67]
Because of the Boxer crisis, Chang attended a "National Conference" (kuo-hui
國會), which was organized by K'ang's follower T'ang Ts'ai-ch'ang 唐才常 (1867-
1900), who was opposed to the war policy of the Manchu government.[68] The
Conference was held in Shanghai on July 26, 1900, attended by approximately
eighty people of reformist and revolutionary backgrounds; Jung Hung (Yung Wing)
容閎 (1828-1912) was elected conference president, Yen Fu, vice president, and
T'ang Ts'ai-ch'ang secretary general.[69] The aims of the Conference were: first,
to protect China's sovereignty, and to create a new independent nation, second,
to claim that the Manchu government had no right to rule over China, and third,
to reinstate the Kuang-hsü Emperor to power.[70] The last goal disturbed Chang;
he denounced T'ang's political ambivalence towards the Manchu government,
asserting that T'ang should not attempt to expel the Manchus on the one hand
and to restore the Kuang-hsü Emperor on the other. Not only did he protest
bitterly the ambiguity of the Conference, Chang also cut off his queue in front of

---

[67]See Hsiao I-shan 蕭一山 , Ch'ing-tai t'ung-shih 清代通史 (Taipei:
Commercial Press, 1962), v. 4, pp. 196-198.

[68]Feng Tzu-yu, Ko-ming i-shih 革命逸史 (Peking: Chung-hua shu-chü,
1979), v. 2, p. 76; The Manchus declared war on the eight foreign nations involved
in the catastrophe, June 21, 1900.

[69]NPCP, v. 1, p. 109; see also Wong, op. cit., p. 25.

[70]NPCP, v. 1, p. 109.

112

those present at the conference.[71] Since the queue was a symbol of Chinese

submission to the conquering Manchus, the action showed his final break with the

Manchu dynasty. He was convinced that the survival of China required the

overthrow of the Manchu regime. He said, "If we do not overthrow the Manchu

government, we can not expect the people to love their own country and to resist

foreign threats. Sooner or later, we will be made slaves of the Europeans and the

Americans."[72] From then on, Chang was committed to anti-Manchu revolution.

While Chang called for revolution to save China, his perception of

"revolution" was only as a means to serve his ultimate goal: the preservation of

China's unique national essence. He said, "If Chinese people do not know the

national essence, China will go the way of India, which has fallen under foreign

rule."[73] In addition, Chang held that Chinese people should find their

revolutionary inspiration in Chinese culture, and "employ the national essence to

stimulate racial spirit and to promote people's patriotism."[74] Chang was also

expressing his further and more fundamental belief that the preservation of the

Chinese national essence gave the nation its mission and meaning. He said:

---

[71]TTNP, p. 7.

[72]Chang, "K'o-ti kuang-miu" 客帝匡謬   in CTYCC, v. 3, p. 120.

[73]Chang, "Hung Hiu-ch'üan yen-i hsü" 洪秀全演義序   in CLHC, v. 1, p. 302.

[74]Chang, "Wo te p'ing-sheng", p. 91.

The reason that a nation is a nation lies in its essence. . . . The difference between humans and the birds as well as the beasts is only because the former can know their past. If the national essence is extinct, people will not know the past of their nation. In this case, what is the difference between them and the birds as well as the beasts. . . . If the people of a nation are not conscious of their own national essence, the nation will be gradually conquered by other nations, and even perish.[75]

Apparently, Chang's devotion to anti-Manchu revolution was mainly as a means to protect China's culture and to guarantee its continuity, for Chang said, "The study of national learning and the overthrow of Manchu rule are exactly the same thing."[76]

After Chang became a revolutionary, he began to revise his book, Ch'iu-shu, an effort which also indicated his conversion from reform to revolution. In the original edition were two essays with clear reformist implications, "K'o-ti" 客帝 (the Guest Emperor) and "Fen-cheng" 分鎮 (Decentralization). The former attempted to justify the Manchu emperor's rule over China and the latter placed a hope in the regional governors-general for reform.[77] The revised book incorporated two essays, "K'e-ti k'uang-miu" 客帝匡謬 (Refuting the Guest Emperor), and "Fen-chen k'uang-miu" 分鎮匡謬 (Refuting Decentralization), to counteract the erroneous views he had presented in the earlier articles. These two essays of refutation

---

[75]Chang, "Yin-tu-jen chih lun kuo-ts'ui" 印度人之論國粹 in CTYCC, v. 4, p. 366.

[76]NPCP, v. 2, p. 828.

[77]See these two articles in CTYCC, v. 3, pp. 65-69 and pp. 72-74.

114

indicated Chang's strong anti-Manchu stance.[78]

Although Chang had become openly a revolutionary, he had no immediate direct connection with any other revolutionary, especially Sun Yat-sen. In August, 1901, Chang went to Soochow 蘇州 , where he obtained a teaching position at Soochow University (Tung-wu ta-hsüeh 東吳大學), a school managed by American missionaries.[79] While Chang was teaching there, he attacked the Manchu government openly, and spread anti-Manchu messages. As a result, the governor of Kiangsu 江蘇 , En Ming 恩銘 (1846-1907) pressed the school authorities and gave orders for the arrest of Chang.[80] In February, 1902, Chang escaped to Shanghai and then to Japan. There he renewed his acquaintance with and began his friendship with Sun. Chang was also in contact with many other revolutionists.[81] In order to advocate racial or anti-manchu revolution and to stimulate a sense of China's history among Chinese students in Japan, Chang in April 1902 proposed a rally to be held in Tokyo in commemoration of the 242nd anniversary of China's fall to the Manchus (Chung-Hsia wang-kuo erh pai-ssu-shih-

---

[78]These two articles are placed as the forward of the revised edition of Ch'iu-shu, which was probably completed in 1902. These articles can be found in CTYCC, v. 3, pp. 116-120 and pp. 120-123.

[79]NPCP, v. 1, pp. 121-122.

[80]TTNP, p. 8.

[81]Ibid., pp. 8-9.

<u>erh nien chi-nien hui</u>　中夏亡國二百四十二年紀念會　　）.[82]　The meeting was

approved by Sun, but prohibited by the Japanese authorities at the request of the

Manchu government. However, the effort did arouse the anti-Manchuism of the

Chinese students in Japan and lead to the founding of many revolutionary

organizations after 1902.[83]

　　　　In July, 1902, Chang returned from Japan to Shanghai, where he taught

Chinese at the Patriotic Academy (<u>Ai-kuo hsüeh-she</u>　愛國學社　) from March,

1903.[84]　The founding of the academy was sponsored by the Chinese

Educational Society (<u>Chung-kuo chiao-yü hui</u>　中國教育會　　), established by

Ts'ai Yüan-p'ei (1876-1940)　蔡元培　　and others in the spring of 1902 in

Shanghai.[85] The members of the society went to Chang's Garden (<u>Chang-yüan</u>

張園　), to speak on revolution openly. Among them, Chang's speeches on

anti-Manchu revolution were especially radical.[86]

　　　　In 1903, Chang wrote a preface to Tsou Jung's　鄒容　　(1885-1905) "Ko-

ming chün"革命軍(Revolutionary Army), in which he fiercely attacked the Manchu

---

[82]<u>Ibid</u>., p. 9.

[83]<u>BDRC</u>, v. 1, p. 93. These revolutionary organizations included the <u>Ch'ing-nien hui</u> 青年會　in 1902, the <u>Chün kuo-min chiao-yü hui</u> 軍國民教育會　in 1902 and the <u>Kuang-fu hui</u> 光復會　in 1904.

[84]<u>NPCP</u>, v. 1, p. 154.

[85]<u>Ibid</u>.

[86]<u>Ibid</u>., p. 159.

government's inability to deal with foreign powers and advocated a revolution to overthrow the Manchu regime.[87] Both Chang's preface and Tsou's pamphlet were published in Su-pao, a newspaper founded in 1896.[88] After Chang Shih-chao 章士釗 (1881-1973) was made editor-in-chief of the Su-pao, the newspaper became radical in tone, and became increasingly a revolutionary paper.[89] The Su-pao also carried Chang's booklet "Po K'ang Yu-wei lun ko-ming shu" 駁康有爲論革命書 (A Letter Refuting K'ang Yu-wei's View on Revolution).

After the failure of the 1898 Reform Movement, K'ang had founded Pao-huang hui 保皇會 (Society to Protect the Emperor). It gained greater support from Chinese intellectuals and the overseas Chinese than Sun Yat-sen's Hsing-Chung hui.[90] In an effort to counter the rising revolutionary movement, K'ang had written an essay against revolution in 1902.[91] K'ang claimed that revolution would require bloodshed and bring only chaos to the nation. Eventually it would lead to foreign intervention and make China the slave of other nations. On the contrary, China could be saved by reform without risking domestic violence and

---

[87]TTNP, p. 9; see also Leung, op. cit., p. 104.

[88]Chiang, op. cit., p. 189.

[89]NPCP, v. 1, p. 166.

[90]See Wong, op. cit., p. 38.

[91]Ibid.

foreign invasion. And reform could be achieved without shedding blood and leaving China in disintegration, only after the Kuang-hsü Emperor regained his power.[92] As for anti-Manchuism, K'ang urged that there was no reason to overthrow the Manchu government, for the Manchus had already been sinicized. This was evident that after the Manchus took over China, they adopted the traditional Chinese culture and system.[93]

Since Kang's influence on intellectuals and overseas Chinese remained very strong, his view on revolution had created an impediment to the rising revolutionary radicalism. Chang, thus, had to refute K'ang's arguments against revolution. In his letter to K'ang, Chang agreed that revolution would shed blood, but he also maintained that reform would require bloodshed as well, as was evident in the collapse of K'ang-Liang's 1898 Reform Movement. In fact, Chang held, "Revolution would be easier to accomplish than reform", for revolution required only leadership, while reform needed both leadership and the people's support. Chang rejected K'ang's argument that revolution would lead to partition of China by foreign powers by indicating that the Manchus were also of foreign origin, and they had already

---

[92]See K'ang, "Ta nan-pei mei-chou chu hua-ch'iao lun Chung-kuo chih k'o hsing li-hsien bu-k'o hsing ko-ming shu" 答南北美洲諸華僑論中國只可行立憲不可行革命書 in CLHC, v. 1, pp. 213-215.

[93]Ibid., v. 1, pp. 220-221; see also Chang "Po K'ang Yu-wei lun ko-ming shu" in Ibid., v. 1, pp. 195-196, and Gasster, op. cit., p. 195.

ceded Chinese territories to other nations.[94] "Since all the Manchus are as stupid
as deer and pigs," Chang said, " can we not launch a revolution?"[95] Chang then
criticized K'ang's readiness to entrust the future of the nation to the timid Kuang-
hsü Emperor, whom Chang ridiculed as "a little clown" (hsiao-ch'ou 小丑) who
"can not distinguish beans from barley."[96] Chang continued to denounce K'ang's
view that the Manchus had already been assimilated by the Chinese. Chang
argued that instead of becoming sinized, the Manchus had already attempted to
assimilate the Chinese as evidenced in the fact that they had forced Chinese
people to adopt their own customs, such as the queue and the Manchu dress.
If the Manchus had not been assimilated by the Chinese, they, as an incompetent
minority race, were not justified to rule the majority Chinese.[97]

　　Chang's and Tsou's radical articles in the Su-pao greatly shocked the
Manchu authorities. The open attack on the entire Manchu race and especially the
denouncement of Kuang-hsü Emperor as a "little clown" brought forth the "Su-pao
case".[98] The Manchu government gave orders to suppress the Su-pao and to

---

[94]Chang, "Po K'ang Yu-wei" in Ibid., v. 1, pp. 201-205; Gasster, op. cit., p. 196.

[95]Chang, "Po K'ang Yu-wei", p. 200.

[96]Ibid., p. 199.

[97]Ibid., pp. 194-200; see also Wong, op. cit., p. 39.

[98]See Chu Hsi-tsu, op. cit., p. 3; see also Wong Young-tsu, Search for Modern
Nationalism, p. 41. On the Su-pao case, see details in Y. C. Wang, "The Su-Pao
Case: A Study of Foreign Pressure, Intellectual Fermentation, and Dynastic

arrest Chang and Tsou in particular. Although they were arrested, the authorities in the Shanghai International Settlement refused the Manchu government's request of extradition. The two were, however, tried by a mixed court of Chinese and foreigners in Shanghai, and Chang was imprisoned for three years and Tsou for two. Both were assigned to the prison in the International Settlement.[99] Tsou Jung died there in April, 1905, just shortly before the end of his term.[100]

While the Manchu government expected that the Su-pao case would curb anti-Manchu sentiments, the result was exactly the opposite.[101] Chang's courage and imprisonment not only made him more famous but also stimulated revolutionary fervor among many of his contemporaries.[102] The Manchu government's failure in attempting to extradite the prisoners was also an indication of its low credibility in dealing with the foreign powers and as a result it lost more prestige in the country.[103] More importantly, before the incident, K'ang's influence on Chinese people was so powerful that his reformism even overshadowed Sun's revolutionary force. However, after the Su-pao case, Sun's

---

Decline", Monumenta Serica, v. 24 (1965), pp. 84-129.

[99]NPCP, v. 1, pp. 170-187; see also BDRC, v. 1, p. 94.

[100]TTNP, p. 10; BDRC, v. 1, p. 94.

[101]See Leung, op. cit., p. 104.

[102]Gasster, op. cit., p. 197.

[103]See Rankin, op. cit., p, p.94

revolutionary cause attracted more Chinese people. Eventually, the revolutionaries became a formidable rival of K'ang and his followers. Revolution then became a political cause powerful enough to challenge K'ang's reformism.[104] In any event, the Su-pao case, not only undermined the Manchu regime, but also made revolution more popular at the time.[105]

Chang's three-year imprisonment was also very important for him both intellectually and politically. During his imprisonment, he started to study Buddhism seriously. For Chang, Buddhism thenceforth was included in Chang's concept of kuo-ts'ui, and was enlisted as a means to promote people's morality for the cause of the revolution. While Chang was imprisoned, he also was involved in the founding of the Restoration Society, which was formed in 1904 with Ts'ai Yüan-p'ei as its president. Chang claimed that he and Ts'ai initiated the idea to establish the Society.[106] When Chang was still in prison, he wrote to Ts'ai urging him and others to organize the society in order to promote anti-Manchu cause.[107] The

---

[104]See Wong, Search for Modern Nationalism, p. 45.

[105]For the significance of the Su-pao case, especially the case of Chang Ping-lin, to the revolutionary movement, see Ibid., pp. 44-46.

[106]NPCP, v. 1, p. 193; see also Ibid., p. 46.

[107]NPCP. v. 1, p. 196; for Chang's involvement in the founding of the Restoration Society, see pp. 196-197.

title of the society, <u>kuang-fu</u> 光復 , was originated by Chang.[108] Later, when T'ao Ch'eng-chang revived the society in 1910, Chang was made its president. Despite their common cause of anti-Manchuism, the Restoration Society then became a bitter rival of the <u>T'ung-meng hui</u>.[109]

After Chang's release from prison on June 29, 1906, he was invited to join the newly founded <u>T'ung-meng hui</u>, the major political organization of the revolutionary camp, and to assume the editorship of the <u>Min-pao</u>, the official organ of the organization. The <u>T'ung-meng hui</u> had been founded on August 20, 1905, with Sun Yat-sen as its chairman (<u>tsung-li</u> 總理). Its purpose was to drive out the Manchus, restore Chinese rule, establish a republic, and equalize land rights.[110] The formation of the <u>T'ung-meng hui</u> rested on the merger of the <u>Hsing-Chung hui</u>, the <u>Hua-hsing hui</u> 華興會 (Society for the Revival of China), the <u>Kuang-fu hui</u> and other splinter groups.[111] During 1905 and 1906 about one

---

[108]The term "<u>kuang-fu</u>" appeared first in Chang's "Ko-ming-chün hsü" 革命軍序 (Preface to the Revolutionary Army). In the preface, Chang said, "To expel the different race (i.e., the Manchus) is called <u>kuang-fu</u> (restoration)". See <u>NPCP</u>, v. 1, p. 197.

[109]<u>Ibid</u>., pp. 318-320.

[110]See Gasster, "The Republican Revolutionary Movement" in <u>The Cambridge History of China</u>, v. 11, p. 491.

[111]See Lee Ta-ling, <u>Foundations of the Chinese Revolution, 1905-1912: An Historical Record of the T'ung-meng hui</u> (New York: St. John's University Press, 1970), p. 25. After the formation of the <u>T'ung-meng hui</u>, however, the <u>Kung-fu hui</u> still remained in existence.

thousand people joined the organization, and a large majority came from the student class of 17 provinces.[112] The membership of the T'ung-meng hui was quite different from that of Sun Yat-sen's earlier Hsing-Chung hui. The latter gained but little support, and even at its height its membership never exceeded 500 in number, most of which came from uneducated people in Kwangtung province.[113] The organization had even excluded students and intellectuals. In contrast, the membership of the T'ung-meng hui was multiprovincial and multiclass. It received new support from students, intellectuals and progressive army officers.[114] By the time of the Wu-ch'ang Uprising in October, 1911, about 10,000 members had joined the T'ung-meng hui and most of its officials were educated.[115]

Although the T'ung-meng hui was a larger and more unified organization than any other revolutionary groups, it was loosely organized. Since the T'ung-meng hui was a conglomeration of different anti-Manchu groups and individuals, not all of its members were of one heart.[116] Most of the rank and file were more

---

[112]See Hsüeh, op. cit., p. 44.

[113]See Mary Clabaugh Wright, "Introduction: The Rising Tide of Change" in China in Revolution: The First Phase, 1900-1913 (New Haven: Yale University Press, 1973), p. 45.

[114]See Hsü, The Rise of Modern China, p. 464.

[115]See Chang Yü-fa, op. cit., pp. 343-349.

[116]Lee Ta-ling, op. cit., p. 39.

involved with their separate organizations instead of the T'ung-meng hui. They remained more loyal to the former and retained keen provincial sentiments.[117] Such provincialism characterized the late Ch'ing and early republican era.[118] While Sun was generally recognized as chairman by the members, his leadership was not unquestioned. This was evident in the internal feud between him and the other leaders of the organization.[119] All these factors hindered the function of the T'ung-meng hui. In addition, while the general headquarters remained in Tokyo, the center of the organization always shifted with Sun Yat-sen himself, wherever he was.[120] Thus, it was actually the personal leadership rather than organizational efforts that was largely responsible for the continuing function and growth of the T'ung-meng hui.

Despite the fact that the T'ung-meng hui was not perfectly effective, its formation did constitute a milestone for the revolutionary movement in China that culminated in the Wu-ch'ang Uprising in October, 1911. While there were many revolutionary groups at one time or another, the T'ung-meng hui was a more

---

[117]See Gasster, Chinese intellectuals and the Revolution of 1911, pp. 55-56; see also Yoshirhiro Hatano, "The New Armies" in China in Revolution: the First Phase, 1900-1913, p. 366.

[118]See Hatano, op. cit., p. 366.

[119]For the personal conflicts within the rank and file of the T'ung-meng hui, see Hsüeh, op. cit., pp. 50-55.

[120]See Lee Ta-ling, op. cit., pp. 39, 205.

unified organization than any others. The T'ung-meng hui was the first organization that could unify the many different anti-Manchu groups and the large number of people with divergent origins and regional aspirations.[121] Although the T'ung-meng hui was loosely organized, it did provide leadership and a central organization to foster the anti-Manchu cause.[122] Above all, with an important common purpose of carrying out a political revolution to overthrow the Manchu government, the T'ung-meng hui did hold together for seven years, and made an important contribution to the Chinese revolutionary movement.[123] After the founding of the organization, revolutionary action was moved ahead quickly, and no less than eight revolts were carried out in South China between 1907 and 1911.[124]

Before Chang assumed the editorship of the Min-pao, the Min-pao had already launched a series of bitter debates with the Hsin-min ts'ung-pao 新民叢報 (New Citizen Journal), an organ of the reformers headed by Liang Ch'i-ch'ao. Although the Min-pao, especially under the editorship of Chang Ping-lin, did bring a large number of students and intellectuals into the revolutionary movement,[125]

---

[121]See Hsüeh, op. cit., p. 45.

[122]See Lee Ta-ling, op. cit., p. 39; see also Hsü, op. cit., p. 465.

[123]Gasster, Chinese Intellectuals, p. 56.

[124]Lee Ta-ling, op. cit., p. iv.

[125]NPCP, v. 1, p. 223; see also Wong, Search for Modern Nationalism, p. 50.

a majority of the students in Japan still favored Liang's reform cause of constitutional monarchy. Thus, in the debate, the Min-pao writers attempted not only to defend their revolutionary cause of republicanism against Liang's constitutional monarchy but also to gain more support from the overseas Chinese. While Chang had challenged K'ang's ideas before, after he took over the Min-pao editorship, his position changed for pragmatic reasons. As the debate with reformists grew, Chang even asserted his colleagues, Hu Han-min and Wang Ching-wei, attacked Liang Ch'i-ch'ao too harshly. This was not because Chang felt sympathy for Liang, despite Chang's earlier friendship, but because, as Chang said, the schism between the revolutionaries and the reformers would only benefit their common enemy, the Manchu government. Chang still hoped that Liang could cooperate with Sun to form a united anti-Manchu front, since Liang had once vacillated between revolution and reform.[126] Thus, when Liang proposed a truce with the Min-pao in January, 1907, Chang accepted Liang's request, but Sun rejected it.[127]

During the Min-pao period, from 1906 to 1908, apart from his expression of strong anti-Manchu views, Chang continued to advocate the preservation of

---

[126]For Liang's vacillation between revolution and reform, see Chang Hao, Liang Ch'i-ch'ao, pp. 220-237; see also Chang P'eng-yüan 張朋園 , Liang Ch'i-ch'ao yü Ch'ing-chi ko-ming 梁啓超與清季革命 (Taipei: Academia Sinica, Institute of Modern History, 1964).

[127]NPCP, v. 1, p. 233.

China's national essence and Buddhism wholeheartedly, which distinguished him from most other members of the T'ung-meng hui.

Although Chang was regarded as a member of the T'ung-meng hui, aside from his anti-Manchu stance, he had little in common with other members of the T'ung-meng hui.[128] Chang's concern for the preservation of the national essence was evident in the fact that he was also a frequent contributor to the National Essence Journal. Chang's focus was different. He believed that the most important mission of the revolution was the preservation of China's unique essence. His sense of history even influenced his methodology. Chang maintained that to accomplish the aim of overthrowing the Manchu government it was a necessity to draw from China's past revolutionary ideas to arouse people's patriotism and foster anti-Manchu sentiment. This approach was evident in his statement that "the overthrow of the Manchu government and the study of the national studies is the same thing."[129] Thus, Chang's revolutionary ideas were derived from "his concern to save the `Chinese essence'".[130] One of the reasons Chang advocated Buddhism was that "Buddhism attaches the greatest importance to equality, and endeavors to remove all obstacles to equality."[131] Since the

---

[128]Lee, op. cit., p. 613.

[129]NPCP, v. 2, p. 828.

[130]See Levenson, op. cit., v. 1, p. 89.

[131]Chang, "Wo te p'ing-sheng", p. 95.

Manchu government discriminated against Chinese people, it thus should be expelled,[132] and Buddhism then could foster the anti-Manchu sentiment.

During the Min-pao period, Chang advocated anti-Manchuism wholeheartedly. Among the members of the T'ung-meng hui, Chang was regarded as the most prominent anti-Manchu proponent. Since Chang had drawn a distinct line between the Manchus and the Han Chinese, and since he fiercely attacked the Manchu government and the Manchu race as a whole, modern scholars tended to regard Chang as a "racist", or an "ethnocentric nativist".[133] However, this was not necessarily the case. Chang's anti-Manchu sentiment was inspired during his childhood. Chang became a revolutionary when this sentiment was reinforced by the failure of K'ang's Reform Movement of 1898 and the Boxer Uprising. Chang called for the overthrow of the Manchus because the government was incapable of preventing foreign invasion. Obviously, Chang's opposition to the Manchus was not confined to simple racism but was inseparable from this anti-imperialism. As he said, " [If one considers revolution] in terms of racial enemies, then the Manchus are our chief enemies not the Europeans and the Americans. In regard to political and social challenges to Chinese, the Westerners are more harmful [to

---

[132]Ibid.

[133]For example, see Charlotte Furth, "The Sage as Rebel: The Inner World of Chang Ping-lin", pp. 117, 138, 149.

128

us Chinese] than are the Manchus".[134] Chang linked the overthrow of the Manchus to resolution of imperialistic threats. Thus, Chang thought that unless the Manchu government was removed, China's struggle with the imperialist countries could not be launched.[135]

Although Chang called for overthrowing the Manchus, his anti-Manchuism was confined to the overthrow of the Manchu government only, rather than to expel it and its people. As Chang said, "To oppose the Manchus is to oppose its imperial household, its officials and its army."[136] He then continued,"To oppose the Manchus is not to oppose all governments and all the Manchu people, but to oppose the Manchu government."[137] He added, though, also non-Manchu people who worked for the Manchu government should be targets of the revolution.

The Dynastic government then was his main target. Even after the success of the Wu-ch'ang Uprising, Chang did not discriminate against the Manchu people but treated them equally to Chinese people. In a letter he wrote to the Manchu

---

[134]Chang, "Ko-ming-chün yüeh-fa wen-ta" 革命軍約法問答   in CLHC, v. 1, p. 432.

[135]See Hu Sheng-wu 胡繩武 and Chin Ch'ung-chi 金沖及 "Hsin-hai ko-ming shih-ch'i Chang Ping-lin te cheng-chih ssu-hsiang" 辛亥革命時期章炳麟的 政治思想 Li-shih yen-chiu 歷史研究 , no. 4 (1961), pp. 5-7.

[136]Chang, "P'ai-Man p'ing-i" 排滿平議 in CTYCC, v. 4, p. 269.

[137]Ibid.

students who studied in Japan, Chang said, "Your [the Manchu] government has been overthrown; while you are Manchus, [you are] also Chinese. Thus, you can get whatever jobs you want, [in] business or agriculture, and your voting rights will be equal to the Chinese."[138] This was the further evidence that Chang was not a ethnocentric nativist or racist.[139] His anti-Manchuism thus meant the overthrow of the Manchu government only. Since the Manchu government was incompetent to defend the nation from foreign aggression, Chang called for revolution to save China. His anti-Manchuism represented an ideological weapon for the republican revolution.

During the Min-pao period, Chang's ideas, when taken together, are considered to be contradictory. He was a classical scholar and yet he criticized Confucianism. And he advocated republicanism, however, he condemned representative government. Much of this appearance of inconsistency, however, is reduced, or even eliminated, if we keep in mind his efforts to preserve the national essence, and his definition of the concept. For all of these differing ideas were perceived by Chang only as a means to serve an ultimate goal: the preservation of the national essence, a concept defined through careful selection. Thus, in terms of his concern for the preservation of the national essence, the

---

[138]Chang, "Chih liu-jih Man-chou hsüeh-sheng shu" 致留日滿洲學生書 in CLHC, v. 1, p. 520.

[139]Wong Young-tsu also argued that Chang was not a racist, see his Search for Modern Nationalism, pp. 62-64.

changes in his ideas are no longer contradictory. Chang was a Confucian scholar, who rejected Confucian morality and even denounced some Confucian ideas.[140] However, in fact, there was not conflict in his thought. In Chang's view, Confucianism was linked with ideas of status and privilege. As he said, "The greatest defect of Confucian is that it makes people pursue wealth and high position."[141] Thus, he continued People who practiced Confucian morality tended to seek wealth and high positions. They can not endure all hardships but pursue their own selfish interests."[142] Nevertheless, Chang also regarded "Confucius as a good historian in ancient times",[143] and praised Confucius' great contributions to Chinese education and history.[144] Moreover, Confucianism also played an important role in China's national essence, which Chang promoted. For example, Confucius and Hsün Tzu were among the philosophers whom Chang admired, and actually Confucian scholars have also made contributions to the chün-t'ien system. Since Chang's acceptance of the Chinese tradition was highly selective, he kept the elements which were essential, and got rid of those that were not. In Chang's eyes, not all of the constituent elements of Confucianism were

---

[140]See Chang, "Chu-tzu-hsüeh lüeh-shuo" in CLHC, v. 1, pp. 289-291.

[141]Chang, "Wo te p'ing-sheng", p. 92.

[142]Chang, "Chu-tzu hsüeh lüeh-shuo", pp. 289-291.

[143]Chang, "Ting-K'ung" in CTYCC, v. 3, p. 135.

[144]Chang, "Po chien-li K'ung-chiao i" 駁建立孔教議　in CLHC, v. 2, p. 690.

essential, and the defect in Confucianism was the idea to pursue wealth and high positions. Because of his concern for preservation of the national essence, Chang praised the essentials in Confucianism and criticized those elements which were not essential in it.

Chang advocated that republicanism was the most advanced from of political organization,[145] however, he condemned representative government.[146] This was because, in Chang's view, Republicanism was consistent with equality. In Chang's eyes, republicanism was the anti-monarchical political institution, which excluded the feature of parliament. Although the form of government Chang preferred was republicanism, he did not accept it without reservation. As he said, "If it is necessary for a nation to have a government, then a republic is probably the least harmful form it can take."[147] Thus, in order to minimize its harmfulness, it needed some amendments: first, equal distribution of land to eliminate tenancy; second, government establish industries to let the workers divide the profits equally; third, a ban on the inheritance of property to prevent wealth from being passed on to descendants; and fourth, to allow the

---

[145]Chang, "Wo te p'ing-sheng",.p. 94.

[146]See Chang, "Tai-i jan-fou lun", pp. 456-470.

[147]CSTS, v. 2, p. 886; see also Gasster, Chinese Intellectuals and the Revolution of 1911, p. 214.

people with the right to remove their representatives from office.[148] After these amendments, Chang saw republicanism as a political system with equality.

Although Chang accepted republicanism, he strongly opposed the idea of introducing representative government into China, for Chang thought, "It is a remnant of feudalism,"[149] which was characterized by a class division between the nobles and the commoners. This division also existed in representative government,[150] for Chang thought that its essential characteristic was "An upper house composed of nobles".[151] Chang asserted that a nation would adopt representative government, only if it was closer to its feudal stage, and still characterized by a division between nobility and commoners.[152] "China, however, had long outgrown her feudal stage", Chang said, "and in China all people are equal."[153] Since the representative government was inconsistent with equality, Chang urged that China should not adopt this system, which was inappropriate for her.[154] According to Chang's conception of the national

---

[148]CSTS, v. 2, p. 886; Gasster, Chinese Intellectuals and the Revolution of 1911, p. 214.

[149]Chang, "Tai-i jan-fou lun", p. 456.

[150]Ibid.

[151]Ibid.

[152]Ibid.

[153]Ibid.

[154]Ibid., p. 470.

essence, all of China's institutions were consistent with equality. Chang denounced representative government, because this institution was incompatible with equality, and was a remnant of feudalism, which was inconsistent with his conception of the national essence.

During the Min-pao period, the Japanese government, at the request of the Manchu government, asked Sun Yat-sen to leave the country in February, 1907. Sun was awarded some money. Before his departure, Sun left a small amount of money for the Min-pao, but took most of his money with him. Chang accused Sun of misappropriating party funds for his personal use.[155] After his conflict with Sun, Chang still edited the Min-pao, however, it was suspended, at the request of the Manchu government, by the Japanese authorities on October 19, 1908.[156] After the closure of the Min-pao, Chang's relationship with the T'ung-meng hui became very tenuous. Even after he was made president of the revived Kuang-fu hui in 1910, Chang remained a member of the T'ung-meng hui until the 1911 revolution. After the success of the Wu-ch'ang Uprising on October 10, 1911, a new China was thus born.[157]

---

[155]Hsüeh, op. cit., pp. 52-53.

[156]NPCP, v. 1, p. 284.

[157]Ibid., p. 351.

CHAPTER 5

CHANG PING-LIN IN THE REPUBLICAN ERA

After the success of the Wu-ch'ang Uprising on October 10, 1911, within a few months, a new Chinese Republic had come into being. In the Republican Era, Chang Ping-lin was still very active in the political arena. However, Chang was portrayed as a "madman" (feng-tzu 瘋子) by both his contemporaries and modern scholars[1] for his nonconformist conduct and his unscrupulous criticism of many of his contemporaries including Sun Yat-sen, Yüan Shih-k'ai and Chiang Kai-shek 蔣介石 (1887-1975), among others. Was Chang really a madman as people suggested? While Chang was a member of the Revolutionary Alliance, he was regarded as an anti-revolutionist in the early Republican Era by his comrades, for in 1911 he had advocated a slogan, "When the revolutionary army rises, the revolutionary parties should be abolished" (ke-ming-chün ch'i, ke-ming-tang hsiao

---

[1]For example, see Furth, "The Sage As Rebel", p. 114; Gasster, Chinese Intellectuals and the Revolution of 1911, p. 190; and Wu Hsiang-hsiang 吳相湘 , "Chang Pin-lin tzu-jen feng-tien" 章炳麟自認瘋顛 , Chuan-chi wen-hsueh 傳記 文學 , 42:4 (April, 1983), pp. 23-32.

(革命軍起，革命黨消).[2] Chang was also regarded as an opportunist because of his changes of political stance.[3] For example, he switched from support of Sun Yat-sen to Yüan Shih-k'ai, and later he denounced Yüan. Was Chang really so changeable? Scholars also suggested that Chang, after 1918, withdrew completely from political activities.[4] Did Chang really disappear from the political scene after 1918?

Chang was considered as the person who attempted to fragment the nation, partially because he advocated a idea of "confederation of autonomous provinces" (lien-sheng tzu-chih 聯省自治) in 1920.[5] Is the suggestion valid? After Sun Yat-sen reorganized the Chinese Revolutionary Party (Chung-hua ke-ming-tang 中華革命黨) he changed its name to Chinese Kuomintang (中國國民黨).[6] In

---

[2]Chang's slogan is stated in his "Chang Ping-lin chih hsiao-mi tang-chien" 章炳麟之消弭黨見 , see NPCP, v. 1, pp. 367-368. For Sun Yat-sen's criticism of this slogan, see Tsou Lu 鄒魯 , Chung-kuo Kuo-ming-tang shih-kao 中國國民黨史稿 . (Ch'ang-sha: Commercial Press, 1938), v. 1, pp. 319-320; For a study of this slogan, see Wang Yu-wei, "P'ing Chang T'ai-yen te `Ko-ming-chün ch'i, ko-ming-tang hsiao'" 評章太炎的革命軍起，革命黨消 , in Chang Nien-ch'ih 章念馳 ed., Chang T'ai-yen sheng-p'ing yü ssu-hsiang yen-chiu wen-hsüan 章太炎生平與思想研究文選 文選 (Chekiang: Jen-min ch'u-pan she, 1986), pp. 109-120.

[3]see NPCP, v. 1, pp. 403-404.

[4]For example, see BDRC, v. 1, p. 96; and Furth, "The Sage As Rebel", p. 114.

[5]For example, see Chiang, op. cit., p. 649. The term lien-sheng tzu-chih was changed from tzu-chih t'ung-meng 自治同盟 by the suggestion of Chang Chi 張繼 , see TTNP p. 43.

[6]See Li Chien-nung, op. cit., p. 542.

order to strengthen the party, the Kuomintang declared its policy of cooperating

with the communists in 1924. However, Chang, in 1925, criticized the cooperative

policy.[7] Why did Chang object to communism? This chapter will discuss and

analyze these and related questions under the heading of Chang Ping-lin in the

Republican Era.

The 1911 Wu-ch'ang Uprising was carried out by the efforts of two

revolutionary groups, the Common Advancement Society (Kung-chin hui 共進會

) and the Literary Society (Wen-hsueh she 文學社).[8] On June 1, 1911, these

two groups agreed to cooperate in a joint action in Wu-ch'ang.[9] The Kung-chin

hui was founded in August, 1907,[10] while the Wen-hsüeh she was established in

January, 1911,[11] the members of the latter were the Ch'ing New Army (hsin-chun

新軍) in Hupeh province.[12] Both organizations were loosely affiliated with the

T'ung-meng hui.[13] This attempt at Wu-ch'ang was quite different from most of

the previous efforts by the T'ung-meng hui, for the former was led by the army

---

[7]See NPCP, v. 2. pp. 828-829.

[8]See Vidya Prakash Dutt, "The First Week of Revolution: The Wuchang Uprising" in China in Revolution: The First Phase, 1900-1913, pp. 383-416.

[9]Hsüeh, op. cit., p. 103.

[10]Ibid., p. 97.

[11]Ibid., p. 96.

[12]Ibid., p. 102.

[13]Li Chien-nung, op. cit., p. 180.

units, while the latter were dominated mainly by the secret societies.[14] However, without the existing problem of the nationalization of railways (t'ieh-tao kuo-yu 鐵 道國有), which served as a stimulus to the uprising,[15] the attempt at Wu-ch'ang probably would not be a quick success.

The problem of railway construction caused the tension between the provincial gentry and the Manchu government in May, 1911. Originally the people of Kwangtung, Hunan, Hupeh and Szechwan were given the right by the government to construct the railways themselves, and the lines in Kwangtung and Szechwan had been under construction. When the central government proclaimed the policy of the nationalization of the railways, and planned to raise funds from foreign loans in order to construct the railways, the people and gentry of the provinces involved protested vigorously, for they saw it as a threat to provincial interests and the invasion of foreign capital. In these provinces the Association for Railway Protection (pao-lu t'ung-chih hui) was organized and the provincial assemblies were planning protests against the central government. Among these provinces, the people and gentry of the Szechwan reacted most bitterly.[16] Thus,

---

[14]Dutt, op. cit., p. 415.

[15]See Chang P'eng-yüan, "The Constitutionists" in China in Revolution: The First Phase, 1900-1913, p. 174.

[16]See Charles H. Hedtke, "The Szechwanese Railroad Protection Movement "Themes of Change and Conflict", Bulletin of the Institute of Modern History, v. 6 (June, 1977), pp. 355-407.

in order to control the unrest in Szechwan province, the Manchu government transferred the troops of Hupeh there, which was an advantage to the revolutionaries in Wu-ch'ang[17] 武昌 . Thus, when the uprising broke out at Wu-ch'ang on October 10, 1911, the revolutionary troops met little resistance, and the governor-general Jui-cheng 瑞澂 fled along with the military commander, Chang Piao 張彪 .[18] By the morning of October 11, the city of Wu-ch'ang was in the hands of the revolutionaries.[19] After the whole of the tri-city of Wuhan had been brought under the complete control of the revolutionary forces on October 12, many provinces responded to the uprising by the declarations of independence of the Manchu government, and the constitutionalists, who dominated the provincial assembly also supported the revolutionists.[20] The success of the Wu-ch'ang Uprising was indeed "accidental", as Sun Yat-sen later recalled, for if Jui-cheng had not fled, Chang Piao certainly would have stayed, and his troops would still have been in order and would have successfully crushed the revolutionary forces.[21]

---

[17]Li Ch'ien-nung, op. cit., pp. 176-177.

[18]See Dutt, op. cit., pp. 402-403.

[19]Ibid., p. 404.

[20]Li Chien-nung, op. cit., pp. 188-189.

[21]Ibid.; see also Hsüeh, op. cit., p. 108.

When the uprising at Wu-ch'ang broke out, Chang Ping-lin was in Japan, where he gave a lecture on Chinese classical studies to his students.[22] Like Sun Yat-sen, Chang was surprised at the success of the uprising, for he was unaware of the attempt at Wu-ch'ang beforehand.[23] After the capture of Shanghai by the revolutionary forces, Chang returned from Japan to Shanghai on November 16, 1911.[24] On November 16, 1911, The People's Independence (Min-li-pao 民立報), an organ of the T'ung-meng hui, announced Chang's return to Shanghai, and its editorial praised him as "the great revolutionary writer" and "a giant among revolutionaries".[25] Chang did play an important role in the period between the Wu-ch'ang Uprising and the founding of the republic. Although the uprising at Wu-ch'ang was a success, the Manchu throne was not overturned until February 12, 1912.[26] Thus, immediate and pressing task, Chang asserted, was that the revolutionaries and the constitutionists should cooperate, regardless of factional and provincial interests, to establish a united government as a basis to fight against their common enemy in the north.[27] The necessity for this was clearest

---

[22]See TTNP, p. 15.

[23]Ibid.

[24]NPCP, v. 1, p. 361.

[25]Ibid.

[26]Ibid., p. 387.

[27]Ibid., pp. 362-363.

following the Wu-ch'ang Uprising, when Chang witnessed violent conflicts not only among the revolutionists and the constitutionists, but also between the revolutionists themselves, particularly between the T'ung-meng hui and the Kuang-fu hui.[28] The conflicts among these groups, Chang observed, was mainly due to the fact that their members identified their partisan interest with national interest, as evidenced in their struggles in seizing power in the provinces.[29] Chang thought that the power struggles among these groups would cause chaos and disunion of the nation and benefit only the Manchu government. Therefore, he urged that both the revolutionaries and the constitutionists should give priority to the national interest over their partisan interest. In these circumstances, Chang advocated the slogan, "The revolutionary army arises, the revolutionary parties should cease to exist." Chang's slogan was also a response to T'an Jen-feng 譚人鳳, a T'ung-meng hui member, who claimed that the new government should be organized under the control of the Revolutionary Alliance.[30] Chang advised that if T'an sought partisan domination of the government, the Revolutionary

---

[28]See Wang, Search for Modern Nationalism, pp. 90-91.

[29]For example, after the capture of Shanghai by the revolutionists on November 4, 1911, there were five commanders (tu-tu 都督) in Kiangsu 江蘇 province. Both Ch'en Ch'i-mei 陳其美 of Revolutionary Alliance and Li Hsieh-ho 李燮和 of Kuang-fu hui claimed as tu-tu, and once struggled in seizing powers in Shanghai. See TTNP, p. 15.

[30]See NPCP. v. 1, p. 367.

Alliance would not gain wide support.[31]   Chang's slogan, however, was misunderstood by the T'ung-meng hui members, and they condemned him as an anti-revolutionist. Even Sun Yat-sen denounced this slogan.

While Chang had severed ties with the T'ung-meng hui, following the Wu-ch'ang Uprising,he was not opposed to it or revolution. In his slogan, the phrase "Ke-ming-tang hsiao" did not refer to the T'ung-meng hui alone, but to all the revolutionary parties, such,as, the Kuang-fu hui, the Kung-chin hui, and the Wen-hsüeh she, among others.[32] The reason Chang proposed this slogan was to promote a united front with all revolutionary parties as a counter to the Manchu dynasty.[33] Chang was afraid that if, after the revolution, these parties would not disband and continued to strengthen their organizations, power struggles among them in the provinces would be inevitable. As a result, the national interest would not be their major concern, for they would place their partisan concerns first. This, Chang worried, would bring about disorder and disunity of the nation, which, in turn, would cause foreign intervention.[34] As a thinker, Chang was not committed to party loyalty or factional interest but committed to the nation.

---

[31]Ibid.

[32]See Wang Yu-wei, "P'ing Chang T'ai-yen te `Ko-ming-chün ch'i, ko-ming-tang hsiao'", p. 116.

[33]Ibid.

[34]See Chang, "Hsüan-yen"宣言 in CLHC, v. 2, p. 527.

Chang's concern seems consistent, and yet his fellows, whose perspective was more political, could easily mistake his position as anti-revolutionary and as opposition to the T'ung-meng hui. Chang's priority derived from his concern for the preservation of the national essence, which he saw as essential for the survival of the nation. As a classical scholar, Chang was concerned also with national survival, however, he gave priority to national heritage or culture over the nation. The latter was important because it was the vehicle for the former.

In order to unite the revolutionaries and the constitutionists, Chang helped found the United Association of Republican China (Chung-hua min-kuo lien-ho hui 中華民國聯合會) on January 3, 1912, and he was elected president of the association.[35] The aim of the association was to unite his contemporaries, regardless of factional and provincial interests, for "assisting and supervising the establishment of the new provisional government."[36] The founding of this association, however, was not an attempt to compete with the T'ung-meng hui or other political groups for power in the newly established government. As president

---

[35]Wang Yu-wei, "P'ing Chang T'ai-yen te `Ko-ming-chün ch'i, ko-ming-tang hsiao', p. 114; See also NPCP, v. 1, pp. 373-376.

[36]NPCP, v. 1, p. 374.

of the association, many of Chang's ideas were presented in its organ, The Great Republican Daily (Ta-kung-ho jih-pao 大共和日報), founded on January 4, 1912.[37]

Chang said, "China was not a newly established country, and many of its fine laws and customs should be retained."[38] Because most revolutionaries and constitutionists favored the borrowing of American or French models for the new government, Chang urged them to value China's customs and conventional institutions.[39] Chang maintained that since the "political systems or institutions of China were formed on the basis of customs", any change of them should be made with reference to China's experience, history and conditions.[40] Chang also asserted that even if any change of political system or institutions for the new government was needed, institutional continuity was imperative. From this point of view, Chang was strongly opposed to the wholesale borrowing of any foreign political system for the newly established provisional government.[41]   Chang's

---

[37]Ibid., p. 377.

[38]Chang, "Chung-hua min-kuo lien-ho-hui ti-i-tz'u yen-shuo tz'u, in CLHC, v. 2, p. 532.

[39]Ibid.; see also Warren Sun, "Chang Ping-lin and His Political Thought", Paper on Far Eastern History (September, 1985) p. 62.

[40]Chang, "Ta-kung-ho jih-pao fa-k'an-tz'u" 大共和日報發刊辭 , in CLHC, v. 2, pp. 537-538.

[41]Ibid.

opposition to slavish borrowing from foreign institutions was not only because he believed the totally different Chinese and foreign political and institutional conditions rendered foreign political models unsuitable for China to follow blindly, but because Chang held that China should retain its cultural and institutional uniqueness.[42] It was Chang's concept of the national essence that he used to define China's uniqueness, and to provide that which the Chinese people could identify with and build their national pride. Thus, in terms of his commitment to the preservation of China's national essence, Chang rejected the wholesale borrowing of any foreign political system as a model for the newly established government. For Chang, any attempt to organize a new government must take its tradition into account. Chang's attitude toward politics or political institutions was manifested in his emphasis on cultural or historical continuity, and respect for tradition.[43]

On March 1, 1912. Chang transformed the United Association of Republican China into the Unification Party (T'ung-i-tang 統一黨), and he was elected as one of its five administrators (li-shih 理事).[44] Although the Unification Party was designated as a political party, strictly speaking, it was not, for its function was to provide the new government with political advice and its aim was

---

[42]Chang, "Chung-hua-min-kuo lien-ho-hui ti-i-tz'u ta-hui yen-shuo-tz'u" pp. 532-535.

[43]Warren Sun, op. cit., pp. 63-64.

[44]NPCP. v. 1, pp. 392-393.

not to seek political power in the government.[45] However, after Chang went to Peking, Chang Chien 張謇 (1853-1926), a constitutionist and an administrator of the Unification Party, and others renamed the Unification Party as the Republican Party (Kung-ho-tang 共和黨), with Li Yüang-hung 黎元洪 as its board Chairman (li-shih-chang 理事長).[46] Chang then realized that Chang Chien and other constitutionists intended to use this consolidation for seeking posts on the cabinet.[47]

Chang was very angry with his associates following their personal interest rather the national interest, and thus he announced that party politics were very harmful.[48] Due to this announcement, Chang was denounced anew by his contemporaries as a madman.[49] Previously, Chang had been portrayed as a madman even before the founding of the Republican China, but the colorful image of Chang as a madman became more widespread in the Republican Era.

The history of the charge about Chang's mental stability began after the Min-pao office had been closed down by the Japanese authorities in 1908, Chang and other Tung-meng hui members in Tokyo were aware that it would not be

---

[45]See Wong, Search for Modern Nationalism, pp. 95-96.

[46]Wang Yu-wei, Chang T'ai-yen chuan, p. 131.

[47]Ibid.

[48]Ibid.

[49]Ibid.

146

published in Japan again. They attempted to publish it in America, but they failed.[50] However, in 1909 when publication was resumed by Wang Ching-wei, with Sun Yat-sen's approval, Chang denounced it as the "fake Min-pao" (Wei Min-pao 偽民報).[51] Chang also accused Sun of misappropriating revolutionary funds.[52]

While Chang's reaction against the reissued journal and Sun's handling of revolutionary funds was rather emotional, his main grievance seems to have been that Sun showed no concern for the Min-pao, the official organ of the T'ung-meng hui, and its crisis.[53] Never did Sun request other revolutionary leaders to help maintain the journal, and after the Min-pao had been closed down he even supported wholeheartedly the founding of the Chung-hsing jih-pao 中興日報 (The Restoration Daily), a newly founded journal in Nan-yang 南洋, the area of Southeast Asia and Indonesia.[54] Chang was angry also because when he was in urgent need of money to maintain the Min-pao, Sun had not given him financial

---

[50]Wong, Search for Modern Nationalism, p. 76; see also Chiang, op. cit., p. 297.

[51]NPCP v. 1, p. 303; see also Wong, Ibid.; Hsüeh, op. cit., p. 54.

[52]Hsüeh, op. cit., p. 54.

[53]See Wong, Search for Modern Nationalism, pp. 76-77; also see Chiang, op. cit., p. 301.

[54]Ibid.; see also Chiang, op. cit., pp. 297, 300.

aid, and had even embezzled revolutionary funds for his personal use.[55] Sun was evidently disturbed by Chang's charge. In defense of Sun, Huang Hsing provided a possible solution to Chang's criticism by portraying Chang as a madman, for no one would take a madman's words seriously.[56]

Even Chang's own statements supported Huang's rhetoric. Chang admitted that he was insane or neurotic (shen-ching-ping 神經病), in the 1906 speech in Tokyo after his release from prison for Su-pao case.[57] However, what Chang meant by shen-ching-ping was his obsession with his agenda and his compulsive quest for the goals or ideals he pursued regardless of his personal interest.[58] Chang's goal was to protect China's national sovereignty, and its cultural heritage. Chang was thus devoted to revolution wholeheartedly, and he had no regret for his involvement in revolution, even though he had been included on the list of those to be apprehended by the Manchu government seven times.[59] However, partly because he portrayed himself as a neurotic, and partly because of his

---

[55]See Hsüeh, op. cit., p. 55.

[56]NPCP, v. 1, pp. 307-308; Wong, Search for Modern Nationalism, p. 77.

[57]See Chang, "Wo te p'ing-sheng" p. 89.

[58]Ibid., pp. 90-91.; see also Wong, "K'ang Yu-wei Chang Ping-lin ho-lun", p. 118.

[59]Chang, "Wo te P'ing-sheng", p. 90. Since the Manchu government was unable to resist the foreign powers, Chang called for revolution to save China. However, revolution was perceived by Chang only as a means to protect China's sovereignty and its essence threatened with extinction from foreign aggression.

outspoken and relentless condemnation of various authorities, Chang was misunderstood by his contemporaries who tended to dismiss him lightly by labelling him as "Lunatic Chang" (Chang-feng-tzu 章瘋子). In fact, not many of his contemporaries were more serious than Chang regarding the national interest. Thus, due to his commitment to national interest, Chang spoke out against whatever he perceived to endanger China's sovereignty and its culture. However this nonconformist deeds and words distinguished him from most of his contemporaries, and they misunderstood him, simply labelling him a madman.

The founding of the Republic of China was announced by Sun Yat-sen on January 1, 1912.[60] In spite of the fact that he had severed ties with the T'ung-meng hui, Chang accepted the invitation of Sun Yat-sen, president of the provisional government in Nanking, to be his privy counselor (Shu-mi ku-wen 樞密顧問).[61] After Yüan Shih-k'ai was elected as provisional president in Peking, he also invited Chang to serve as his senior adviser (Kao-teng Ku-wen高等顧問).[62] However, Chang later publicly denounced Yüan. When a military government was formed in Canton in 1917 with Sun Yat-sen as its generalissimo (ta-yüan-shuai 大元帥), Sun appointed Chang secretary-general (mi-shu-chang 祕書長) of the

---

[60]NPCP, v. 1, pp. 372-373.

[61]TTNP, p. 17.

[62]Ibid., p. 18.

government.[63]

Chang's changes of political stance suggested to some that he was a political opportunist. However, Chang's changing attachments to various political authorities did not represent a change or departure from the main concern of his thinking; these several political masters were but agents for carrying out Chang's goals of preserving China's national sovereignty and its culture.[64] In fact, Chang was not a political opportunist but a scholar who had strong commitment to China's national interest and its cultural heritage.

In spite of his connections with the Restoration Society, Chang did not turn down the post offered by Sun as his privy counselor. However, his relations with the T'ung-meng hui and the provisional government became strained when he denounced Sun's mistaken decision to accept Japanese funding of the Han-yeh-p'ing Mines;[65] Sun had reacted to the provisional government's urgent need of funds by granting part of the Han-yeh-p'ing Mine to the Japanese company in exchange of a loan of five million yen. Chang publicly denounced this decision

---

[63]See NPCP, v. 1, p. 569.

[64]See Lee, op. cit., p. 619.

[65]NPCP, v. 1, pp. 386-387; See also Chiang, op. cit., pp. 544-545; Lee, op. cit., p. 620.

and urged Sun to cancel the deal, for Chang thought that the sale of iron and coal mines to a foreign country would only undermine China's sovereignty.[66] The deal was finally canceled because public opinion was seething with indignation, and thus the Board of Directors of the Han-yeh-p'ing Mine company disapproved the deal.[67]

Chang's observation that Sun's provisional government in Nanking performed very poorly marked Chang's growing distrust for the revolutionaries' first rebuplican structure. When he discovered that Sun's government was too incompetent and incapable to unify the nation, Chang gradually shifted his support toward Yüan Shih-k'ai.[68] Like most revolutionaries and constitutionists, Chang thought Yüan was an able man who was capable of maintaining national order and unity, and of precluding foreign intervention because his military force was strong enough to dethrone the Manchus and to crush the revolution.[69] Thus, supporting

---

[66]See Chang, "Pu-kao fan-tui Han-yeh-p'ing ti-ya chih chen-hsiang" 布告反對 漢冶萍抵押之眞相 , in CLHC, v. 2, pp. 560-561; TTNP, pp. 17-18; See also Wong, Search for Modern Nationalism, p. 92.

[67]See Chiang, op. cit., pp. 544-545; Wong, Search for Modern Nationalism, p. 92.

[68]For the study of Yüan shih-k'ai, see Ernest P. Young, The Presidency of Yüan Shih-k'ai: Liberalism and Dictatorship in Early Republican China (Ann Arbor: The University of Michigan Press, 1977).

[69]See James E. Sheridan, China in Disintegration: The Republican Era in Chinese History, 1912-1949. (New York: The Free Press, 1975), p. 48.; See also Wong, Search for Modern Nationalism, pp. 92-93.

Yüan as the president seemed to be the best option at that time for the unsettled republic. Otherwise Chang was afraid of foreign intervention in the event of prolonged civil war. Chang's support of Yüan, however, was not because of Yüan's character but because Chang thought that Yüan was strong enough to bring the country together.[70] Obviously, it was Chang's belief that Yüan was the agent who was able to carry out Chang's goal of preserving China's national sovereignty that enabled Chang to support him. Yüan Shih-k'ai was inaugurated as provisional president of the Republic on March 10, 1912, and Yüan appointed Chang as his adviser in April. In the winter of 1912, Chang resigned from this post and Yüan appointed Chang as the Frontier Defense Commissioner of the Three Eastern Provinces and Chang accepted it.[71] Chang's interest in Manchuria was mainly due to his concern for the frontier crisis of the time. Since the Wu-ch'ang Uprising in 1911, with China in disorder, the frontiers were in crisis.[72]

In 1912 a series of threats from Japan and Russia existed in both Mongolia and Manchuria. These two foreign powers attempted to extend their influence in Chinese frontier regions. The Japanese government even planned to carry out

---

[70]Chang, "Ching-kao tui-tai chien-tieh che" 敬告對待間諜者 , in CLHC, v. 2, pp. 570-571.

[71]TTNP, p. 20.

[72]See Chiang, op. cit., pp. 563-565; See also Wong, Search for Modern Nationalism, p. 99.

colonizing projects in south Manchuria. In February, the Russian forces occupied Hulunbeier in northern Manchuria, while Japanese troops were stationed in Mukden (Shenyang 瀋陽) in Manchuria. In July, the two foreign powers signed an agreement to partition Inner Mongolia, and the Russian government also demanded the Republic recognize the independence of Manchuria. Such actions called the security of Chinese frontiers into serious question.[73]

Before November, Chang accepted the post of Frontier Defense Commissioner offered by Yüan; he had paid a visit to Manchuria in October, 1912.[74] Since national sovereignty and unification were Chang's major concerns and since his support of Yüan's presidency was mainly because he thought Yüan was able to defend China's sovereignty, which included frontier provinces, Chang's acceptance of the post was obviously due to his intention to secure Chinese frontiers.[75]

Chang left Peking for Ch'ang-ch'un in Manchuria to take up his appointment, where he set up his Frontier Defense Commissioner agency in Spring, 1913.[76] After a brief stay in Manchuria, however, Chang discovered that

---

[73]See Wong, Search for Modern Nationalism, p.99; Chiang, op. cit., pp. 563-565.

[74]Chiang, op. cit., p. 564.

[75]Wong, Search for Modern Nationalism, pp. 99-100.

[76]TTNP, p. 20.

the position was no more than a title.[77]   And he was unable to carry out his projects in Manchuria because of shortage of funds.[78] In April, 1913, when he heard that Sung Chiao-jen had been assassinated in Shanghai on March 20, 1913, apparently by Yüan's agents, Chang left Manchuria for Shanghai.[79]

Yüan's assassination of Sung was due to political reasons.[80]   In December, 1912, the Nationalist Party (Kuomintang 國民黨) had won the majority of seats in both houses of the new parliament. As the acting chairman of the party, Sung would possibly be the new prime minister. For Yüan, Sung was a real threat to his position, because if Sung were prime minister, he would challenge his presidency. This was the reason underlying Yüan's assassination of Sung.[81]

Sung's death crushed Chang's confidence in Yüan's presidency and his government[82]. He then joined Sun Yat-sen, Huang Hsing and other old T'ung-meng hui members in publicly denouncing Yüan Shih-k'ai. At a meeting held by the Kuomintang, Chang accused Yüan of betraying the Republic, since he did not use his army against foreign powers but used it instead to suppress his political

---

[77]BDRC, v. 1, p. 95.

[78]TTNP, p. 21.

[79]NPCP, v. 1, p. 426; See also BDRC, v. 1, p. 95.

[80]Chiang, op. cit., pp. 570-571.

[81]Ibid.

[82]Wong, Search for Modern Nationalism, p. 108.

rivals.[83] In order to punish Yüan for the Sung assassination, Sun Yat-sen and his followers launched the "Second Revolution" (erh-tz'u ke-ming 二次革命) on July 12, 1913, aiming at crushing Yüan's power.[84] However, the revolution was suppressed by Yüan's troops,[85] and Sun had to flee abroad, because he was condemned by Yüan as a rebel.[86]

In early August, 1913, Chang set out for Peking to reorganize the Kung-ho-tang, which he had previously headed.[87] He arrived at the headquarters of the party on August 11, and on the following day he was placed under house arrest by Yüan. Only his closest friends and disciples were permitted to visit him.[88] This was because Yüan was afraid that Chang's criticism of him would stir up people's opposition to his rule of the country.[89]

Chang was not released from Yüan's confinement until Yüan's death in June, 1916.[90] These three years' confinement was not so physically unpleasant

---

[83]NPCP, v. 1, pp. 436-437.

[84]Ibid., p. 427.

[85]Ibid.

[86]Chiang, op. cit., p. 584.

[87]TTNP, p. 24.

[88]BDRC, v. 1, p. 95.

[89]Ibid.

[90]TTNP, pp. 26-27.

as that of 1903-1906 in Shanghai because of the Su-pao case, however, the mental suffering was indeed more severe, for Chang did not know when he would be released and he also worried about the future of the republic that he had helped create, under Yüan's rule.[91] Chang attempted more than once to escape from Peking, but in vain.[92] He then went on a hunger strike, and prepared to die.[93] As he prepared for death, he sighed, "Much to his chagrin, he was to die after the republic had founded even though he had survived the anti-Manchu war."[94] Moreover, he was also concerned about Chinese culture, as he predicted, "China's cultural heritage would become extinct with him."[95] Chang's hunger strike, however, ended, mainly because of the persuasion of his friend, Ma Hsü-lun 馬敍倫 (b. 1884).[96]

During the confinement, Chang published the final edition of Ch'iu-shu and renamed and published it as Chien-lun in 1915. Many of his writings on revolution,

---

[91]Wong, Search for Modern Nationalism, p. 112.

[92]See NPCP, v. 1, pp. 467, 523.

[93]Ibid., pp. 473-474.

[94]Ibid, p. 474; See also Wong, Search for Modern Nationalism, p. 113.

[95]NPCP, v. 1, p. 474.

[96]Chiang, op. cit., p. 607.

collected in Ch'iu-shu were deleted.[97] In the Chien-lun, Chang, however, added many of his writings on national studies instead.[98] In the same year, Chang also published his collected works, Chang-shih ts'ung-shu 章氏叢書 (The Collected Writings of Chang Ping-lin).[99] Many of the works, considered as Chang's most important writings on Chinese classics and philology, were included in the ts'ung-shu.[100] Almost all the works collected in the ts'ung-shu were those on national studies, and many of his political essays were excluded from it.[101] Although major articles from the Min-pao were retained, they were placed merely in such section as pieh-lu 別錄 (supplementary record) of his collected essays (wen-lu 文錄). Chang's intention to collect mainly his scholarly works thus was obviously an attempt to preserve those writings that he regarded as of durable scholarship.

---

[97]For example, in Chien-lun Chang deleted two articles, "K'o-ti kuang-miu" and "Fen-chen kuang-miu", which were originally included in Ch'iu-shu., see NPCP, v. 1, p. 488.

[98]Ibid.

[99]Ibid., p. 510.

[100]They are, for example, Hsin Fang-yen (New Dialects), Wen-shih (Origins of Chinese Writing), Hsiao-hsüeh ta-wen (Answers to Questions on Philology). Kuo-ku lun-heng (Essays on National Heritage), Ch'i-wu lun-shih (An Interpretation of Discourse on the Equality of All Things'), and Chuang-tzu chieh-ku (Textual Commentaries on Chuang-tzu).

[101]See Lu Hsün 魯迅 , Lu Hsün ch'üan-chi 魯迅全集 (The Complete Works of Lu Hsün), (Shanghai: Jen-min ch'u-pan-she, 1981), v. 6, p. 547.

Chang was released on June 8, 1916, two days after Yüan's death.[102]   The

death of Yüan shih-k'ai marked the opening of the "warlord period", an era of

chaos in republican China from 1916 to at least 1928.[103] On September 1, 1917,

a military government was formed in Canton with Sun Yat-sen as its generalissimo;

Chang Ping-lin was made secretary-general of the government.[104] The purpose

of organizing the government was to support   the constitution protection

movement (hu-fa-yün-tung 護法運動) against the Peking government, then under

the control of Tuan Ch'i-jui 段祺瑞   , a follower of Yüan shih-k'ai.[105] Although

the military government was under his control, Sun had no military force, except

for a small navy[106]. In order to gain support for the government from powerful

militarists in Yunnan 雲南 , Chang went to K'un-ming 昆明 , where he met T'ang

Chi-yao 唐繼堯   , the commander of Yunnan, and the most powerful militarist in

southwest China at that time.[107]   Chang's mission to persuade T'ang to

cooperate militarily with Sun's government against the Peking government,

---

[102]NPCP, v. 1, p. 525.

[103]See Sheridan, op. cit., p. 57.

[104]NPCP. v. 1, p. 569.

[105]Ibid.

[106]Li Chien-nung, op. cit., p. 434.

[107]NPCP. v. 1, p. 570; See also Chiang, op. cit., pp. 634-635.

however, failed. On October 11, 1918, when Chang returned to Shanghai, he found that Sun had resigned from his position in the military government.[108]

After 1918, Chang remained very active in the political arena rather than retreating from political activism as some scholars suggested.[109] This was evident in his involvement in the movement for the confederation of autonomous provinces in the 1920s and in the campaign against Japanese aggression in the 1930s.

Chang did not advocate the idea of the confederation of autonomous provinces until the constitution protection movement failed.[110] The idea of confederation of autonomous provinces was not in vogue until after 1920, however, it was not a new idea for the Chinese people in the 1920s.[111] In the late 1890s, leaders of both reformist and revolutionary camps had already fostered this idea.[112] In 1900, Liang Ch'i-ch'ao suggested that the Swiss federal system might be used as a model for new China.[113] The revolutionaries, however, favored the

---

[108]BDRC, v. 1, p. 96.

[109]For example, BDRC, v. 1, p. 96; Furth, "The Sage As Rebel" p. 114.

[110]Wong, Search for Modern Nationalism, p. 121.

[111]Ibid., p. 120.

[112]Ibid.

[113]See Liang, Yin-ping-shih ch'üan-chi 飲冰室全集 , (Peking: Chung-hua shu-chü, n.d.), v. 24, p. 209.

federal system of the United States as the model for the future China.[114]

Nevertheless, this idea was not carried out right after the founding of republic, because at that time China was still in chaos.[115]

Since the founding of the republic, Chang had supported centralization.[116] However, even the central government under Yüan's rule was unable to unify the nation. Chang attributed the failure of national unification to the result the abuse of power by the central government.[117] His distrust for centralization then grew. After Yüan's death, political chaos remained or was even worse. Since neither the Peking nor the Canton governments had the strength to unify the entire nation, Chang advocated the confederation of autonomous provinces, which Chang thought might be the best way at the time to achieve national unification.[118]

Chang explained his ideas on the confederacy as follows: each province was permitted to be autonomous, to make its own constitution, and to deal with its own domestic affairs.[119] In this way, provincial governments would not

---

[114]See "Min-sheng chu-i yü Chung-kuo ke-ming chi ch'ien-t'u" in Min-pao, no. 4, p. 106.

[115]See Wong, Search for Modern Nationalism, p. 120.

[116]Ibid., p. 116.

[117]Chang, "Lien-sheng tzu-chih hsü-chih cheng-fu i" 聯省自治虛置政府議 in CLHC, v. 2, p. 752.

[118]Ibid., pp. 752-753.

[119]Ibid.

interfere with each other. After each provincial assembly had completed its constitution, a new constitution for the confederate government could be made by representatives from each provincial assembly.[120] Chang then proposed that confederation should be completed in three consecutive stages: provincial autonomy, multi-provincial autonomy, and a confederate government of autonomous provinces.[121] In the first stage, each province should draft its constitution and establish its autonomy. Several autonomous provinces could then cooperate with one another for their common interests. Finally, all the autonomous provinces could establish a confederate government.[122] In this way it was expected that the chaotic warfare of the warlords might be stopped and the goal of national unification might be achieved.[123]

Chang's advocacy of the confederation of autonomous provinces, however, has drawn some criticism from scholars who regarded him as a separatist and his idea as an attempt to promote the cession of provinces from China. This was because they linked Chang with some warlords who used this idea to justify their

---

[120]Chang, "Mi-lun tsai ch'ü san-du shuo" 弭亂在去三蠹說 , in CLHC, v. 2, pp. 756-759.

[121]See NPCP, v. 2, pp. 609-610.

[122]Ibid.; see also Wong, Search for Modern Nationalism, pp. 121-122.

[123]Chang, "Lien-sheng tzu-chih hsü-chih cheng-fu i" pp. 752-753.

occupation of various territories.[124] However, this criticism was not valid. Chang had advocated the confederation of autonomous provinces only after he found that political centralism had failed to solve China's serious political problems in the early republican era. He maintained that the republic suffered from disunity and disorder because of the failure of centralization.[125] Thus, he advocated the confederation of autonomous provinces as a scheme to replace the early model of political centralism and as a means to achieve a new style of national unification.[126] Chang stressed that his advocacy of the confederacy was because he believed it would better serve the national interest.[127] Thus, he openly denounced some warlords who used their military forces to occupy territories in order to disunite the nation.[128] However, the movement for the confederation of autonomous provinces finally failed, because the Peiyang warlords, attempting to seize political powers, sought a military solution for national unification, and because the Kuomintang also attempted to unify the nation.[129]

---

[124]Li Chien-nung, op. cit., p. 461.

[125]Chang, "Lien-sheng tzu-chih hsü-chih cheng-fu i" pp. 752-753.

[126]Chang, "Ko-sheng tzu-chih kung-pao ch'üan-kuo ling-t'u shuo" 各省自治共保領土說 in CLHC, v. 2, pp. 754-755.

[127]Ibid.

[128]See Chiang, op. cit., pp. 644-646.

[129]Ibid., p. 647; see also Wong, Search for Modern Nationalism, pp. 123-124.

After the reorganization of the Kuomintang in January, 1923, the party sought national unity. The Kuomintang also opposed the idea of the confederacy for it was regarded as an obstacle to national unification under its leadership.[130] The Kuomintang also declared its policy of accepting communists as members and making an alliance with Soviet Russia (lien-O jung-kung 聯俄容共).[131] The purpose of the Kuomintang's cooperation with the communists was an attempt to strengthen its party in order to destroy warlordism and to establish a strong national government that could resist foreign powers.[132]

Chang, however, openly denounced the cooperative policy, and was thus associated with the anti-communist movement.[133] Chang opposed sovietization (ch'ih-hua 赤化)[134] because he was afraid of the expansion of Soviet Russia's influence to China, and that sovietization would then threaten China's sovereignty and its unique culture.[135] Chang also objected to communism because it was alien in origin and because the Chinese Communist Party was a party supported

---

[130]Li Chien-nung, op. cit., pp. 556-559.

[131]Ibid., pp. 546-550.; See also Sheridan, op. cit., pp. 141-146.

[132]See Sheridan, op. cit., pp. 141, 146.

[133]NPCP, v. 2, pp. 778-779.

[134]In general, "Ch'ih-hua" meant both sovietization and communization.

[135]NPCP, v. 2, pp.828-829; see also Wong, Search for Modern Nationalism, p. 129.

by a foreign power, Soviet Russia.[136] He believed that the communist's take-over of China would be a national disaster.[137] On April, 28, 1926, an Anti-Communist Alliance for Saving the Nation (Fan-ch'ih chiu-kuo ta lien-ho hui 反赤救國大聯合會) was inaugurated, with Chang as its chairman.[138] Its aim was "to counter sovietization and communism in an attempt to save the nation."[139] They asserted, "If sovietization or communism was wide-spread in China, eventually Soviet Russia would control China."[140] Obviously, Chang's opposition to communism was an attempt to protect China's sovereignty and its culture.

Even during the early 1930s Chang did not withdraw from the political arena because of the grave national crisis brought about by the Japanese aggression.[141] The Mukden incident of September 18, 1931 compelled Chang to rise to action.[142] Since Chang was concerned for the protection of China's sovereignty and its territory, Chang hoped that the Nanking government, then

---

[136]NPCP, v. 2, p. 828.

[137]Ibid., p. 861.

[138]Ibid., pp. 860-861.

[139]Ibid., p. 861.

[140]Ibid.

[141]Ibid., p. 912.

[142]Ibid., pp. 915-916; see also Chiang, op. cit., p. 673.

under the rule of Chiang K'ai-shek would stand up to the Japanese invasion.[143]
When the Nanking government failed to make an immediate military response,
Chang openly condemned it for failing in its responsibility to defend the nation.[144]
Without gaining support from the government to resist Japanese aggression,
Chang placed his hope in General Chang Hsüeh-liang 張學良, who then headed
Manchuria. In February, 1932, Chang made a trip to Peking, where he met the
General and urged him to resist the Japanese.[145] However, his effort was in vain.
Chang was deeply distressed, and he went back to Soochow in the autumn of
1932.[146] During his final years from 1931 until his death on June 14, 1936,
Chang devoted most of his time and energies to teaching and research on
Chinese classics and philology, by which Chang sought to preserve China's
unique cultural heritage.

---

[143]Chang, "Yü Ma Hsiang-pao, Shen En-fu lien-ho hsüan-yen" 與馬相伯，沈恩孚聯合宣言, in CLHC, v. 2, pp. 834-835.

[144]Chang, "Chih Ma Tsung-huo shu" 致馬宗霍書, in CLHC, v. 2, pp. 826-827.

[145]BDRC, v. 1, p. 96.

[146]NPCP, v. 2, p. 922.

CHAPTER 6

CHANG PING-LIN AND THE MODERN
CHINESE CULTURAL CONSERVATISM

While Chang Ping-lin was regarded as a political radical, for his eminence as a strong anti-Manchu revolutionist, he can be also described as a conservative, or more precisely a cultural conservative. If "to conserve "means" to keep in safety, or from harm, decay or loss",[1] then the efforts made by Chang to preserve China's essence as a reaction to imperialism and westernization is certainly conservatism. Here "the conservative" maybe denotes one whose attitude attaches greater importance to the preservation of the tradition than to innovation and change.[2]

Although Chang was described as a conservative, he never opposed the notion of change or innovation. Nevertheless, Chang maintained that the change should not cause the loss of contact with one's cultural past or one's tradition. Chang believed that China should retain its cultural uniqueness, for without this uniqueness, China could not maintain its national identity. Thus, after the founding of the republic, which he helped to establish, Chang was engaged in building China as a modern nation. Nevertheless, Chang asserted that the building of the

---

[1]C.T. Onions, ed., The Oxford Universal Dictionary of Historical Principles (Oxford: Oxford University Press, 1955), p. 375.

[2]See Philip P. Wiener, ed., Dictionary of the History of Ideas (New York: Charles Scribner's Sons, 1973), v. 1, p. 477.

nation should take its tradition into account. Thus, Chang was opposed to the slavish borrowing of any foreign model for the new republic, for he feared that China might become an imitation Western nation, its cultural uniqueness could not be retained, and its national identity would be lost. In short, in terms of his concern for the preservation of the national essence, Chang did not oppose change, but favored change with continuity.

In twentieth-century China, modern Chinese conservatism is characterized by the fact that it is not basically a political conservatism; rather it is mainly cultural conservatism which is rarely linked to any commitment to the prevailing political order.[3] Chang and many other cultural conservatives were quite definite about which elements of China's cultural heritage should be maintained,[4] although they were quite politically innovative to find institutions to serve their cultural goals.

Chang's commitment to the preservation of the national essence was shared by others, as in the case of the so-called National Essence Movement. Cultural conservatism constituted an important element in efforts to counter wholesale westernization in early Republican Era; the New Culture Movement (Hsin-wen-hua yün-tung 新文化運動), taking place generally between 1917 and 1923, came into being as one response to the cultural conservatism of the national

---

[3]See Benjamin I. Schwartz, "Notes on Conservatism in General and in China in Particular" in The Limits of Change, p. 16.

[4]Ibid.

essence groups.[5] Three different but related organizations formed the national essence groups: the Society for the Protection of National Studies (Kuo-hsüeh pao-ts'un hui 國學保存會) founded in 1904; the Southern Society (Nan-she 南社) founded in 1909; and the Critical Review Society (Hsüeh-heng 學衡) founded by the Southeastern University (Tung-nan ta-hsüeh 東南大學) faculty in 1922.[6]

Although Chang and these conservative intellectuals used the same term, national essence, their perceptions of this concept were not quite the same. Moreover, Chang's thought reflects an important dimension of the intellectual change in twentieth-century China, for it illustrates the tension between political and cultural ideals among the elite of his generation, particularly among the national essence intellectuals.

This chapter will analyze the similarities and differences between Chang's concept of the national essence and the ideas of other national essence groups. In addition, Chang's role in modern Chinese cultural conservatism is examined in the historical context of the development of modern China, and its significance is also measured.

---

[5]See Bernal, "Liu Shih-p'ei and National Essence" in The Limits of Change, p. 112.

[6]See Laurence A. Schneider, "National Essence and the New Intelligentsia" in The Limits of Change, p. 58.

The concept of kuo-ts'ui did not derive from the traditional vocabulary but had come into being as a response to the Western impact and as a reaction against westernization. Chang Ping-lin was the first scholar-revolutionary to put forth the term of kuo-ts'ui in 1903. He adopted the Japanese neologism kokusui (kuo-ts'ui) to replace Chang Chih-tung's t'i, a term used in his famous t'i-yung dichotomy. Although Chang Chih-tung himself even used the concept of kuo-ts'ui on occasion to refer to Chinese essence, his perception of this concept was different from Chang Ping-lin's.

Chang Chih-tung's concept of kuo-ts'ui was basically confined to Confucianism, particularly the teachings of Confucius and Mencius, for he intended to defend the Confucian doctrines rather than China's entire cultural heritage.[7] In a sense, Chang Chih-tung tended to equate China's cultural tradition with Confucianism; the latter was regarded as the country's orthodox doctrine and was a state philosophy officially sponsored by the Ch'ing government. As a scholar-official of the government, Chang Chih-tung also attached himself to Confucianism. Although Chang Chih-tung did not reject the Ch'ing Han Learning School, he did criticize it as excessively scholastic.[8] Thus, it was no surprise that Chang Chih-tung was impatient with the study of philology,[9] an essential discipline in the

---

[7]See Wang Erh-min, op. cit., pp. 84-85.

[8]Schneider, op. cit., p. 64; see also Ayers, op. cit., pp. 53-54.

[9]Schneider, Ibid.

tradition of Han Learning. Chang Chih-tung also regarded the study of pre-Ch'in noncanonical texts as potentially subversive,[10] only because it was unorthodox. Chang Chih-tung's effort to preserve the Confucian doctrine was mainly as a means to protect the monarchy and was due to his deep commitment to the political order of the time.

By contrast, Chang Ping-lin defined the concept of the national essence more broadly than Chang Chih-tung did. Unlike Chang Chih-tung, Chang Ping-lin was committed deeply to Han Learning, which not only formed the foundation of his scholarship but also opened doors for him to all the dominant alternatives to orthodox Chinese thought.[11] Chang Ping-lin did not believe that the whole Chinese cultural tradition was a monolithic unit but, instead, a complex of many contending tendencies.[12] Although he asserted that Confucianism had contributed significantly to the formation of the Chinese cultural heritage, he rejected the equation of Confucianism with Chinese culture. He also emphasized the contributions of pre-Ch'in noncanonical texts to the Chinese culture, and thus engaged in the study of these texts. The study of pre-Ch'in noncanonical texts then gradually became Chang Ping-lin's primary research interest, and he also made great contribution to the study of these texts.

---

[10]Ibid.

[11]Chang Hao, Chinese Intellectuals in Crisis, p. 117.

[12]Schwartz, op. cit., p. 17.

Unlike Chang Chih-tung, who did not favor the study of philology,[13] Chang Ping-lin's greatest accomplishments in the field of classical learning were probably his studies of philology.[14] In the tradition of Han Learning, philology was at first regarded as an essential tool for the study of classics, but then grew into a major field of study.[15] As a Han Learning scholar, Chang Ping-lin was devoted to the study of philology. He asserted that the Chinese language embodied in itself the entire history of Chinese culture[16] and that "philology was the foundation of national study."[17] Chang Ping-lin has published a number of works on philology.[18] From the tradition of Han Learning, Chang Ping-lin adopted the school's methodology on the study of philology, however, he also widened its content and broke new ground.[19] And philology constituted as a major element in his concept of kuo-ts'ui.

Chang's concern for the preservation of the national essence was not to defend the dynasty, as with Chang Chih-tung, but to contribute to the survival of

---

[13]Schneider, op. cit., p. 64.

[14]See BDRC, v. 1, p. 97.

[15]See Liang, op. cit., "Bibliography", p. x.

[16]Chang, "Wo te p'ing-sheng", p. 97; Furth, "The Sage as Rebel", p. 125.

[17]Chang, "Hsiao-hsüeh lüeh-shuo" 小學略說 in CSTS, v. 1, p. 421.

[18]For example, Hsin Fang-yen, Wen-shih and Hsiao-hsüeh ta-wen.

[19]Liang, op. cit., p. 111.

the nation, for he believed that the preservation of the national essence would strengthen the nation. Chang's first promotion of the national essence was a response to two major intellectual and cultural crises: the western impact and K'ang Yu-wei's interpretation of Chinese culture, as discussed before. During the Republican Era, Chang took up the defense of the national essence again. This time his defense was due to the rising skepticism among New Culturists towards traditional culture.[20]

The New Culture Movement was launched in 1917 by the new intellectuals, Western-trained or Western-influenced. The main aim of the movement was to regenerate the nation. After the founding of the republic, China was still in chaos. Even the adoption of parliament, constitution and party politics had not brought peace, order and unity to the nation. In fact, the new republic was endangered by warlordism and intensified foreign imperialism. In the midst of such chaos, Chinese intellectuals with growing anxiety sought some means to save the nation[21] and generally took the position that vast and fundamental changes were imperative to rejuvenate. They advocated a radical change in the intellectual foundations of the nation and accepted the Western culture as the basis of a new order. In this regard, they called for a critical reevaluation of traditional culture in

---

[20]See Chu Tsu-keng, op. cit., p. 6.

[21]See Chow Tse-tsung, The May Fourth Movement: Intellectual Revolution in Modern China, p. 41.

the light of Western science and democracy.[22] They also launched a literary revolution (wen-hsüeh ke-ming 文學革命) to adopt the vernacular language (pai-hua 白話) instead of classical or literary language (wen-yen 文言) in writing.[23] The iconoclastic attitude of the new intellectuals toward China's past dealt tradition a deadly blow.

The movement was reinforced by the return of some Chinese intellectuals from abroad. Among them, Ch'en Tu-hsiu 陳獨秀 (1879-1942),[24] Ts'ai Yüan-p'ei[25] and Hu Shih 胡適 (1891-1962)[26] were the most prominent.[27] Ch'en returned from Japan in 1915, and his founding of the New Youth (Hsin Ch'ing-nien 新青年) marked the beginning of the movement.[28] Ts'ai, returning from France in 1916, took over as chancellor of the National University of Peking, and

---

[22]Ibid., p. 173.

[23]Ibid., pp. 269-271.

[24]For the study of Ch'en Tu-hsiu, see Thomas C. Kuo, Chen Tu-hsiu (1879-1942) and the Chinese Communist Movement (New Jersey: Seton Hall University Press, 1975), and Feigon Lee, Chen Duxiu: Founder of the Chinese Communist Party (Princeton: Princeton University Press, 1983).

[25]For Ts'ai, see William J. Duiker, Ts'ai Yüan-pei: Educator of Modern China (Philadelphia: Pennsylvania University Press, 1977).

[26]For the study of Hu Shih, see Jerome B. Grieder, Hu Shih and the Chinese Renaissance: Liberalism in the Chinese Revolution, 1917-1937 (Cambridge: Harvard University Press, 1970).

[27]See Chow, The May Fourth Movement, p. 41.

[28]Ibid.

he carried out many practical reforms in the university. Among his innovations, the most significant was that he encouraged freedom of opinion and invited scholars of divergent beliefs to teach at the university. This policy of freedom in education made possible an alliance of the new intellectuals.[29] Hu Shih returned from the United States in 1917, and joined the leadership of the movement.[30] He had already initiated the literary revolution in 1915.

During the New Culture Movement, iconoclasm and a critical spirit prevailed among most of the new intellectuals. One effect of this iconoclastic attitude towards China's cultural heritage was reflected, after 1919, in the reevaluative study of Chinese classics and history.[31] The origin of this new movement was the New Culture Movement, although a similar reexamination had occurred in K'ang Yu-wei's interpretations of the classics.[32] K'ang in his work, Hsin-hsüeh wei-ching k'ao 新學偽經考 (A Study of the Classics Forged during the Hsin Period) published in 1891, claimed that all the Ancient Text classics had been forged by a Han scholar, Liu Hsin. His purpose was to provide the ideological foundation for Wang Mang's usurpation of the Han throne, and for the institutional reforms

---

[29]Ibid., pp. 48-51.

[30]Ibid., p. 41.

[31]Ibid.

[32]Ibid., pp. 314-315.

proposed by Wang.[33] In 1897, K'ang published his <u>K'ung Tzu kai-chih k'ao</u> 孔
子改制考 (A Study of Confucius as Reformer). In this book, K'ang argued that
all the Six Classics had been written by Confucius himself, and that the long-
standing view that Confucius had merely edited them was wrong.[34] K'ang also
asserted that Confucius had attempted to justify his institutional reforms with the
cloak of antiquity, relying on such ancient sage-kings as Yao 堯 (2357?- 2256?
B.C.) and Shun 舜 (2255?- 2206? B.C.).[35] Not only Confucius, K'ang claimed,
but all the ancient thinkers, such as Lao-Tzu 老子 and Mo-Tzu 墨子 , had
advocated institutional reforms on the basis antiquity.[36] After the appearance of
these two books, the truth of the classical canon, which had been regarded as
sacred and inviolable for the past several thousand years, was now cast into
doubt.[37] In this regard, it seemed that all the ancient books had to be
reexamined and reappraised.[38] Although K'ang's interpretations were mainly for
the purpose of his institutional reform, his skepticism in classical studies greatly

---

[33]Chang Hao, <u>Liang Ch'i-ch'ao and Intellectual Transition in China, 1890-1907</u>,
p. 48; see also Liang, <u>op</u>. <u>cit</u>., p. 92.

[34]Liang, <u>Ibid</u>., p. 94.

[35]<u>Ibid</u>.; see also Chang Hao, <u>Liang Ch'i-ch'ao</u>, pp. 49-50.

[36]Liang, <u>Ibid</u>.; Chang Hao, <u>Liang Ch'i-ch'ao</u>, p. 49.

[37]Liang, <u>Ibid</u>., p. 95.

[38]<u>Ibid</u>., p. 93.

influenced the young scholars and prompted a critical and skeptical attitude towards their cultural heritage.[39]

In the 1920s, a group of "antiquity doubters" (i-ku p'ai 疑古派) emerged in the study of Chinese history and classics, led by Ku Chieh-kang 顧頡剛 (b. 1893),[40] Ch'ien Hsüan-t'ung 錢玄同 (1887-1939), and Hu Shih.[41] Among them, Ku was probably the most prominent. Under the influence of Hu Shih, Ku extended Hu's agnostic and genetic methods to study ancient Chinese philosophy, and ancient Chinese history.[42] In 1922, Ku was engaged in the study of the legend of Emperor Yü 禹 .[43] According to his research, Emperor Yü, 'ho had been regarded as one of the ideal sage kings, was but a legendary figure.[44] However, Ku was not satisfied with this result. He then made an attempt to use a linguistic approach to the study of Emperor Yü. Based on the ancient dictionary, Shuo-wen chieh-tzu 說文解字 (Explaining Primary Graphs and Analyzing Derived Graphs), edited by Later Han scholar, Hsü Shen 許慎 (58-147), Ku proved that

---

[39]Chow, The May Fourth Movement, p. 315.

[40]For the study of Ku, see Schneider, Ku Chieh-kang and China's New History: Nationalism and the Quest for Alternative Traditions (Berkeley: University of California, 1971.).

[41]Chow, The May Fourth Movement, p. 316.

[42]Ibid., pp. 315-316.

[43]Ibid., p. 316.

[44]Ibid.

Emperor Yü was a reptile (p'a-ts'ung 爬蟲).[45] Ku's methodology and conclusion were criticized by historians later.[46]

As the rising skepticism prevailed in the intellectual world in the 1920s, Chang Ping-lin rose again to defend China's essence. Chang's defense was mainly a reaction to this wave of "antiquity doubters".[47] He claimed that the skeptical attitude and approach toward China's past would tear the accepted version of China's history to pieces.[48] He then assumed the responsibility to resist the tide of the time, and claimed that his commitment was to revere national history.[49]

Chang had formulated his concern for the preservation of the national essence in 1903, an act which also greatly influenced the formation of the national essence clique (kuo-ts'ui p'ai 國粹派) in 1904 when Liu Shih-p'ei and Huang Chieh 黃節 (1874-1935) founded the Society for the Protection of the National Studies, and the next year founded its organ, The National Essence Journal.[50] At the time when the society was founded, Chang was still in prison; the effort was

---

[45]See Schneider, Ku Chieh-kang and China's New History, pp. 226-227.

[46]Chow, The May Fourth Movement, pp. 316-317.

[47]See Chu Tsu-keng, op. cit., p. 6.

[48]Ibid.

[49]Ibid.

[50]See Schneider, Ku Chieh-kang and China's New History, p. 34.

stimulated by Chang's "Personal Statement [made] in Prison in 1903" (K'uei-mao yü-chung tzu-chi 癸卯獄中自記), in which Chang formulated his concern for preserving and glorifying China's cultural heritage.[51] The Journal also carried Chang's "Personal Statement".[52] Probably also under Chang's influence, the initial title of the Society was Kuo-ts'ui hsüeh-she 國粹學社 (the Society for [Preserving] National Essence). Even during his imprisonment, Chang was the major contributor to the journal. The national essence movement was later reinforced by Chang's release from prison in 1906, for he then helped stimulate the intellectual fervor for classical studies among Chinese intellectuals.[53]

By 1904, the idea of the preservation of the national essence became current among Liu and his national essence society.[54] The aim of the Society for the Protection of National Studies was to preserve China's essence, which the national essence advocates regarded as essential for national survival, for they claimed that national culture or essence was the foundation of a nation.[55] They

[51]See Fan, op. cit., pp. 71-72.

[52]Ibid., p. 72.

[53]Bernal, "Liu Shih-p'ei", p. 110.

[54]Ibid., p. 104.

[55]See Yang T'ien-shih 楊天石 , "Lun Hsin-hai ke-ming ch'ien te kuo-ts'ui chu-i ssu-ch'ao" 論辛亥革命前的國粹主義思潮 in Chung-kuo Chin san-pai-nien hsüeh-shu ssu-hsiang lun-chi 中國近三百年學術思想論集 v. 5, p. 37.

asserted that if the national culture were extinct, the nation would go with it.[56] Thus, they gave priority to the preservation of national essence over the protection of the nation. They believed that in China's past the nation had been preserved from extinction by foreigners mainly because of the continuation of its great cultural tradition.[57] Thus, they maintained the idea that the survival of the nation depended on the survival of its essence. They cited examples to support their assertion. After Egypt and India were destroyed by England, they never restored themselves, because they had failed to maintain their individual national essences.[58] The fall of the Sung dynasty to the Mongol was because it adopted Mongol customs.[59] While China had been taken over in the past, as by the Mongols, the strength of its essence had permitted it to restore itself.[60] They also cited Japan and Germany as examples of successful revival.[61]

In order to preserve the national essence, the Society's scholars set up a library to keep rare books and other treasures of Chinese culture.[62] These

---

[56]Ibid.

[57]Schneider, Ku Chieh-kang and China's New History, p. 35.

[58]Ibid., p. 38.

[59]Bernal, "Liu shih-p'ei", p. 105.

[60]Schneider, Ku Chieh-kang and China's New History, p. 38.

[61]Ibid.; see also Bernal, "Liu Shih-p'ei", p. 105.

[62]Yang, op. cit., p. 36; Bernal, "Liu Shih-p'ei", p. 104.

treasures were carried in the Journal.[63]   Scores of books from the library's holdings were also reprinted and circulated on the market.[64]   The Society also established the Academy for [Preserving] the National Essence (<u>Kuo-ts'ui hsüeh-t'ang</u> 國粹學堂) in Shanghai, where national essence scholars could lecture to the young generation.[65]

Since the scholarly foundation of the national essence advocates lay in the tradition of Han Learning, they adhered to the School of Han Learning.[66]   Under the influence of the school, they regarded Confucius as only one of the pre-Ch'in philosophers.[67]   They emphasized the study of non-Confucian schools, which they regarded as even preeminent over Confucianism.[68]   They saw pre-Ch'in noncanonical philosophers as representatives of a period of Chinese spiritand vitality and as the equivalents of their contemporaries, the classical Greek philosophers.   Thus, they attempted to revive the classical non-Confucian philosophy.[69] And they believed that the refinement of this classical philosophy

---

[63]Bernal, <u>Ibid</u>.

[64]Schneider, "National Essence and the New Intelligentsia", p. 65.

[65]<u>Ibid</u>.; Yang, <u>op</u>. <u>cit</u>., p. 36.

[66]Schneider, <u>Ibid</u>., p. 64.

[67]Bernal, "Liu Shih-p'ei", p. 106.

[68]Furth, "Culture and Politics in Modern Chinese Conservatism" in <u>The Limits of Changes</u>, p. 36.

[69]Bernal, "Liu Shih-p'ei", p. 106.

would make China a nation of wealth and power.[70] Like Shiga, a Japanese national essence scholar, who favored the aesthetic definition of the kokusui, the national essence advocates also regarded the Chinese arts as elements of the national essence, and a great number of illustrations of paintings and calligraphy were carried in the National Essence Journal.[71]

In defining the concept of the national essence, the national essence scholars were different from Chang Ping-lin. The meaning of China's essence for them was even broader than for Chang. Their efforts to define the national essence came very close to wholesale, indiscriminate affirmation of China's entire cultural heritage.[72]

Chang's definition of the national essence, however, did not go as far as Liu's national essence group did, for his promotion of the national essence was definitely not a type of indiscriminate preservation. For Chang, the concept of the national essence did not equate with China's entire cultural tradition. In Chang's eyes, not all the elements in traditional culture were essential. Chang's acceptance of the cultural heritage thus became a matter of deliberate choice. Therefore, Chang's concept of the national essence included mainly those essential elements

---

[70]Ibid.

[71]Ibid., p. 106.

[72]Yang, "Lun Hsin-hai ke-ming ch'ien te kuo-ts'ui chu-i ssu-ch'ao", pp. 40-41; Chang Hao, Chinese Intellectuals in Crisis, p. 119.

in China's cultural heritage. Chang believed that only after the refinement of China's cultural heritage could China's culture be equivalent to, if not superior to, Western culture, and then China could meet the challenge from the West.

In 1909. Liu Ya-tzu柳亞子(1887-1958), Kao Hsü 高旭 (1887-1925) and Ch'en Ch'ü-ping 陳去病 (b. 1883) organized a literary club, the Southern Society.[73] When the society was initially established, it had only seventeen members.[74] However, by 1930s its membership numbered more than 1,000.[75] Although the Southern Society had recruited a large numbers of members, it was loosely organized.[76] The society met formally only twice a year,[77] and published twenty-two anthologies of its members' poetry and prose, the Nan-she ts'ung-k'o 南社叢刻.[78]

---

[73]See Shen Sung-ch'iao 沈松僑 , Hsüeh-heng-p'ai yü wu-ssu shih-ch'i te fan Hsin-wen-hua yün-tung, p. 23; Schneider, "National Essence and the New Intelligentsia", p. 62. For the study of Nan-she, see Liu Ya-tzu, Nan-she chi-lüeh 南社紀略 (Taipei: Wen-hai ch'u-pan she); Yang T'ien-shih and Liu Yen-ch'eng 劉彥成 , Nan-she 南社 (Peking: Chung-hua shu-chü, 1980); Cheng I-mei 鄭逸 梅 , ed., Nan-she ts'ung-t'an 南社叢談 (Shanghai: Jen-min ch'u-pan-she, 1981); Liang Hui-ching 梁惠錦 , "Nan-she: Ch'ing-mo Min-ch'u te ke-ming wen-i t'uan- t'i" 南社—清末民初的革命文藝團體 Chung-kuo li-shih hsüeh-hui shih-hsüeh chi-k'an 中國歷史學會史學集刊no. 12, pp. 247-261.

[74]See Cheng, op. cit., p. 1.

[75]Ibid.

[76]Ibid.; Schneider, "National Essence and the New Intelligentsia", p. 62.

[77]Cheng, Ibid., pp. 9-10; Schneider, Ibid.

[78]Cheng, Ibid.; Schneider, Ibid.

Strictly speaking, the Southern Society lacked a formal platform,[79] however, its general aim was to employ literature, especially traditional poetry, to promote the national spirit, which was essential for the survival of the nation.[80] But the national spirit, the Nan-she members claimed, lay in national studies, or more precisely in China's literary tradition. Thus, they had to preserve the national heritage. As one of the Nan-she leaders, Kao Hsü stated clearly:

> A nation with its spirit (hun 魂) will survive; a nation without it will perish. However, where does the national spirit lie? It is in national study. Thus, preserving national spirit must start by preserving national studies.[81]

Similarly, another member of the society, Hsü Chih-heng 許之衡, stated "National spirit originates from national study. If national study is extinct, where does the national spirit lie?"[82]

Since most members of the Southern Society were poets, they devoted themselves to the study and practice of traditional literature, especially poetry and tz'u 詞 ,[83] as is evident in the anthologies of the society.[84] Most works

---

[79]Schneider, Ibid.

[80]Cheng, op. cit., p. 10; Liu Ya-tzu, op. cit., p. 93.

[81]See quote in Yang, "Lun Hsin-hai ke-ming ch'ien te kuo-ts'ui chu-i ssu-ch'ao", p. 42.

[82]See quote in Shen, op. cit., p. 23.

[83]See Schneider, Ku Chieh-kang, p. 40. Tz'u is a traditional type of lyric verse characterized by varied tonal patterns and lines of irregular length.

[84]See the brief account of Nan-she ts'ung-k'an in Cheng, op. cit., pp. 75-88.

collected in the anthologies were traditional poetry or tz'u. The concept of national essence held by the Southern Society was basically linked to the field of traditional literature. However, Chang's concept of the national essence would not be narrowly confined to traditional literature only.

The Southern Society and Liu's national essence group had overlapping memberships with the Revolutionary Alliance.[85] In fact, apart from their devotion to the preservation of the national essence, many national essence advocates were involved in pre-1911 anti-Manchu activities and revolution.[86] Both literary societies offered anti-Manchu propaganda for the revolutionary cause aiming at overthrowing the Manchu monarchy and establishing a republic.[87] Like Chang Ping-lin, these national essence advocates were placed in a state of tension between political radicalism and cultural conservatism. However, they, too, perceived radical politics as a means to fulfill an ultimate goal of the preservation of China's essence.[88]

Their radicalism was a response to two related problems of the time. Firstly, they were reacting to the corruption of Chinese traditional culture and values by

---

[85]Cheng, op. cit., pp. 1-3.

[86]See Schneider, "National Essence and the New Intelligentsia", pp. 60-63.

[87]Ibid., p. 63.

[88]Ibid., pp. 60-61; 69-70.

184

the Manchu government.[89] Liu Shih-p'ei and Huang Chieh, for example, strongly implied that the Manchus defiled Chinese culture.[90] They then called for a distinction between the Han Chinese and the barbarians, i.e. the Manchus, and promoted anti-Manchuism by the way of scholarly activities.

Secondly, it was a response to the challenge of the West.[91] Under pressure from Western powers, they were afraid that China was threatened with extinction, and Chinese would lose their national identity.[92] But because the Manchu government was unable to defend the nation, they called for revolution to save China. Nevertheless, much of the work of these two literary societies was directed mainly at keeping Chinese traditional culture alive.[93] This was because the national essence advocates believed that traditional culture or national essence was the foundation of a nation, and was essential for its survival.[94] Moreover, their devotion to the promotion of the national essence was reinforced by the idea that the preservation of the national essence would strengthen the nation.[95]

---

[89]Bernal, "Liu Shih-p'ei" pp. 95-96, 104; Schneider, "National Essence and the New Intelligentsia", pp. 69-70.

[90]Bernal, Ibid., pp. 104-105.

[91]Schneider, "National Essence and the New Intelligentsia" p. 69.

[92]Ibid.

[93]Ibid., p. 63.

[94]Yang, "Lun Hsin-hai ke-ming ch'ien te kuo-ts'ui chu-i ssu-ch'ao", p. 37.

[95]Bernal, "Liu Shih-p'ei", p. 103.

During the Republican Era, the national essence advocates took up the defense of the national essence again. This time their defense was a reaction against the anti-traditionalism and the wave of wholesale westernization in the New Culture Movement.[96] In an effort to oppose the wave of westernization in the movement, Liu Shih-p'ei and Huang K'an even established a journal, The National Heritage (Kuo-ku 國故) to advocate Confucianism, traditional literature and ethics.[97] They held that westernization would destroy the national essence and Chinese culture identity.[98] They also objected to employing the vernacular language in literary writing.[99]

Although the national essence advocates asserted an idea that Western learning could be employed to illuminate Chinese learning, this idea was merely another expression of Chang Chih-tung's t'i-yung formula, as evident in their expression: "National essence is basically the study of spirit; `Europeanization' [Western learning] is basically the study of form."[100] In fact, they never attempted to syncretize these two cultures. That would have to wait for the Hsüeh-

---

[96]Shen Sung-ch'iao, op. cit., pp. 24.

[97]Ibid., p. 25.

[98]Ibid., pp. 24-25.

[99]Ibid., pp. 26-27.

[100]Schneider, Ku Chieh-kang, pp. 38-40.

186

<u>heng</u> advocates who made an effort to implement a kind of syncretism to fuse Chinese and Western cultures.[101]

<u>Hsüeh-heng</u> was founded in 1922 by Mei Kuang-ti 梅光迪 (1890-1945), Wu Mi 吳宓 (b. 1894) and Hu Hsien-su 胡先驌 (b. 1893), faculty members of the Southeastern University.[102] Mei, Wu and Hu were founders and the most prominent members of the <u>Hsüeh-heng</u> group. All of them were associated with the previous national essence groups.[103] Wu was a disciple of Huang Chieh, a co-founder of the Society for the Protection of National Studies.[104] As early as 1915, Mei and Hu had been members of the Southern Society.[105] Mei and Wu were among the few Chinese who had majored in Western literature at that time, and under a prominent Western literary scholar, Irving Babbitt.[106] Hu also studied at Harvard University, and was regarded as a follower of Babbitt.[107]

---

[101]Schneider, "National Essence and the New Intelligentsia", pp. 65-66.

[102]Shen Sung-ch'iao, op. cit., p. 73. For the study of <u>Hsüeh-heng</u> clique, see Shen, op.cit.; Richard Barry Rosen, "The National Heritage Opposition to the New Culture and Literary Movements of China in the 1920s" (Ph.D. Dissertation, University of California, Berkeley, 1969).

[103]Shen Sung-ch'iao, op. cit., p. 82.

[104]Ibid.

[105]Ibid.

[106]Rosen, op. cit., p. 21.

[107]Ibid.

The primary aim of the Hsüeh-heng was to promote national essence, and to fuse Chinese culture with Western culture.[108] According to Mei, the purpose of his founding Hsüeh-heng was "to expound and advocate traditional culture, and to introduce new learning, i.e. Western learning."[109] However, the iconoclastic anti-traditionalism rising in the New Culture Movement made the Hsüeh-heng group put much emphasis on the defense of national essence.[110] Although both Hsüeh-heng advocates and the New Culturists were engaged in the introduction of Western culture to China, their purposes were different. In the eyes of the New Culturists, Western culture and Chinese traditional culture were incompatible, and thus they attempted to replace Chinese culture wholly by Western culture. In this regard, anti-traditionalism and wholesale westernization characterized the New Culture Movement.[111] In contrast, Western culture was perceived by the Hsüeh-heng clique as a means to protect Chinese traditional culture.[112] Thus, when the New Culturists attacked traditional culture without reservation, the Hsüeh-heng advocates rose to defend it.

---

[108]Shen Sung-ch'iao, op. cit., p. 74.

[109]Ibid.

[110]Ibid., pp. 74-75.

[111]Ibid., pp. 81-82.

[112]Ibid.

The Hsüeh-heng scholars not only adopted the true Western culture to illuminate Chinese culture, but also attempted to create a new culture by synthesizing both Chinese and Western essences. They insisted that the central core of the Chinese tradition lay in Confucianism. However, they held that culture had not national boundary, though each culture developed from its own historical experience. In this sense, they thought that Confucian tradition was not only China's cultural essence, but also part of world culture. In Confucianism, they found universal elements as the West's true tradition did. For the Hsüeh-heng group these universal elements in both cultures thus provided the intellectual link between the cultural heritages of China and the West. Thus while Chang Ping-lin and other national essence scholars regarded Chinese cultural heritage as China's cultural uniqueness, the Hsüeh-heng scholars promoted Confucian tradition in universal terms. Nevertheless, they all rejected the anti-traditionalism of the New Culture Movement.

The New Culture Movement brought prominence to the new literary movement, or the Vernacular Movement (Pai-hua-wen yün-tung 白話文運動). Hu Shih, the leading exponent of the Vernacular Movement, attempted a literary revolution, which was to employ vernacular language as a substitute for classical language in literary writings.[113] The Hsüeh-heng group, however, opposed Hu's literary revolution. When Hsüeh-heng was founded, in its brief statement of

---

[113]Rosen, op. cit., p. 20.

regulations (Chien-chang 簡章), it stated very clearly that "the aim of Hsüeh-heng was to oppose vernacular language in writings."[114] Thus, the Hsüeh-heng advocates insisted on using classical language in their writings.[115] Although Mei agreed that a literary reform was necessary, he opposed Hu's drive to abandon classical language and adopt vernacular language in writing.[116] Mei held that if the literature in China was to be written in the vernacular language, a style not within the mainstream of the Chinese literary tradition, then the very foundations of the Chinese cultural heritage would be destroyed.[117] However, the defense of classical language by the Hsüeh-heng group was ineffective, because the vernacular language certainly became China's national language.[118]

Hsüeh-heng was disbanded in 1933, mainly because of personnel and financial problems.[119] However, the fundamental reason was that the Hsüeh-heng scholars all wrote in classical language, so their writings were not widely read, and thus they gained not wide support.[120] Nevertheless, in the 1920s the

---

[114]Shen Sung-ch'iao, op. cit., p. 152.

[115]Ibid.

[116]Ibid., p. 89.

[117]Rosen, op. cit., p. 25.

[118]Shen Sung-ch'iao, op. cit., p. 120.

[119]Ibid., p. 84.

[120]See Chow, The May Fourth Movement, p. 282; Shen, op. cit., p. 240.

Hsüeh-heng clique was the only national essence group in a position to challenge the wave of wholesale westernization and the Vernacular Movement. Although Hsüeh-heng and the other two national essence groups failed to survive in the 1920s, their efforts to defend China's essence against westernization could not be easily dismissed. In the wave of westernization, they helped shape the idea of the national essence, and to retain Chinese cultural identity.

In modern Chinese cultural conservatism, Chang Ping-lin was undoubtedly the most influential and prominent scholar. His commitment to the preservation of the national essence foreshadowed the National Essence Movement in the early Republican Era. Chang also helped foster the National Essence Movement after 1905. Thereafter, the idea of the preservation of the national essence became the most important theme of the modern Chinese cultural conservatism.

Chang's concept of the national essence consisted of those elements essential in China's cultural heritage. In terms of this concept, Chang could never accept the idea that all the China's past was evil as advocated by the New Culturists, nor did he accept the idea of indiscriminate preservation of China's cultural heritage maintained by Liu's national essence group. Chang would also disagree with the Southern Society scholars who narrowly confined the concept of the national essence to the field of literature. Chang's concept of the national essence implied that there were other different but equal national essences.[121]

---

[121]See Bernal, "Liu Shih-pei", p. 103.

Chang had a conviction that each nation had its own cultural uniqueness. Without this uniqueness, no nation could maintain its cultural identity.[122] Since China's past was also unique, any attempt to eliminate this uniqueness in the name of universals was bound to be disorienting.[123] Thus, with the rise of anti-traditionalism and wholesale westernization in the New Culture Movement, Chang came to defend strongly China's national essence, for he was afraid that China could not maintain its cultural uniqueness, and its national identity would then be lost. By the same token, Chang objected to the uncritical transplantation of foreign models for the new republic.

Chang's commitments to the preservation of the national essence, to retaining China's cultural uniqueness, and its cultural identity were the most consistent and fundamental threads in Chang's life, through which Chang contributed significantly to the modern Chinese cultural conservatism. Chang's commitments inspired the national essence clique, who then assumed their responsibilities to defend China's cultural heritage and to retain its cultural identity in the face of wholesale westernization in the New Culture Movement. Even the Hsüeh-heng group also endeavored to preserve China's national essence and to maintain China's cultural identity, though their view of culture differed greatly from

---

[122]See Wong, Search for Modern Nationalism, p. viii.

[123]Sun, op. cit., p. 63.

Chang's, for they advocated the idea that culture had not national boundary.[124]

Thus, the efforts to preserve China's essence and its identity were the most

important mission for Chang and the national essence clique. They not only

defended China's cultural heritage against westernization, but also sought to

preserve those values in China's past that endured. In this regard, modern

Chinese cultural conservatism had its significance, for it provided an alternative for

an understanding of the intellectual changes in the history of modern China.

---

[124]Wong, Search for Modern Nationalism, p. 145.

CHAPTER 7

CONCLUSION

Shortly after Chang Ping-lin's death on June 14, 1936, Lu Hsün, probably Chang's best known disciple, wrote two short essays to assess him.[1] Lu Hsün concluded, "I think that his contribution to the history of revolution is greater than that to the history of scholarship."[2] In praise of Chang's contributions to revolution, Lu wrote that he heard about Chang not because of his great accomplishments in the fields of classical studies and philology, but because he refuted K'ang Yu-wei's ideas against revolution, was then involved in the Su-pao case, and was imprisoned in the International Settlement in Shanghai for three years.[3] Lu continued that he liked to read The People's Journal, edited by Chang, not because of his writings in dense classical style, but because of Chang's campaigns against Liang Ch'i-ch'ao who advocated constitutional monarchy.[4]

---

[1]They are "Kuan-yü T'ai-yen hsien-sheng erh-san-shih" 關於太炎先生二三事 collected in Chang Nien-ch'ih, ed., Chang T'ai-yen sheng-p'ing yü hsüeh-shu 章太炎生平與 學術 (Hong Kong: San-lien shu-tien, 1988), pp. 8-10; and "Yin T'ai-yen hsien-sheng erh hsiang-ch'i te erh-san-shih" 因太炎先生而想起的二三事 in Lu Hsün Ch'üan-chi 魯迅全集(Shanghai: Jen-min ch'u-pan-she, 1981), v. 6, pp. 556-561.

[2]See Lu Hsün, "Kuan-yü T'ai-yen hsien-sheng erh-san-shih" p. 8; Leung, op.cit;, p. 108; Wong, Search for Modern Nationalism, p. 143.

[3]Lu Hsün, Ibid., p. 8.

[4]Ibid., p. 9.

Lu Hsün also mentioned that although Chang has realized his goal of overthrowing the Manchu government, two things that Chang regarded as the most important were merely impractical fantasy: firstly, to employ religion to promote the people's faith and morality; secondly, to use the national essence to stimulate racial character and to promote patriotic fervor.[5] Lu Hsün was disappointed that Chang deleted the anti-Manchu articles from his collected works, the Chang-shih ts'ung-shu, in which many of his important scholarly works on classical studies, and philology were included.[6] Lu's disappointment was because he regarded these anti-Manchu articles as the greatest and lasting accomplishments in Chang's life.[7]

Lu Hsün's comment upon Chang was important, for it exerted a great influence upon later assessments of Chang by modern scholars.[8] Nevertheless, it was not an accurate assessment of Chang, for Lu Hsün was too obsessed with his own beliefs. After the New Culture Movement, Lu became an anti-traditionalist and was regarded as a progressive revolutionary.[9] Therefore, he praised Chang's contribution to revolution, but intended to belittle the value of Chang's classical

---

[5]Ibid., p. 9.

[6]Ibid., p. 10.

[7]Ibid; Wong, Search for Modern Nationalism, pp. 142-143.

[8]Wong, Ibid, p. 142.

[9]Ibid.

scholarship and the significance of his <u>kuo-ts'ui</u> idea. Lu was unaware that Chang deleted those anti-Manchu articles because they were too shallow to be included in his collected works. Due to his concern for preserving China's essence, Chang, instead, collected most of his important scholarly works on national studies in the <u>Chang-shih ts'ung-shu</u>. His intention was obviously an attempt to preserve these writings that he regarded as of durable scholarship.

Lu also failed to understand that the preservation of the national essence was the most fundamental idea in Chang's thinking, from which he derived his revolutionary inspirations and political ideas. Revolution or politics was perceived by Chang merely as a means to fulfill his ultimate goal of preserving China's cultural heritage. In Chang's career, revolution or politics were interludes, while the preservation of China's essence was a lifelong calling.

Although Chang had been exposed to anti-Manchu sentiments during his childhood, he had first become a reformer rather than an anti-Manchu revolutionary. This was because at that time Chang regarded reformism as the most effective means to deal with China's political crisis. More importantly, Chang supported K'ang Yu-wei's reform program because he shared K'ang's concern to preserve China's traditional culture, for throughout his life the preservation of China's cultural heritage was Chang's ultimate concern or goal, and he perceived reform as a means to fulfill this goal.

While Chang was a supporter of K'ang's reformism, he denounced K'ang's idea of establishing Confucianism as a state religion due to their doctrinal differences. However, Chang's objection to K'ang's interpretation of Confucianism did not represent a revival of the debate between the New Text and Ancient Text Schools as scholars suggested. Under the influence of his teacher Yü Yüeh, a late Ch'ing master of Han Learning, Chang's intellectual tendency was to draw on the scholarships of both of these two schools. Although Chang claimed to be an advocate of the Ancient Text School in 1891, he still adopted New Text ideas in his writings. Even after he became a reformer, he still continued to employ New Text ideas in articles written for the Shih-wu Pao, a reformist journal. Thus, Chang's criticism of Kang's views on Confucianism did not suggest a revival of the debate between these two schools as scholars have suggested. And Chang's objections to K'ang's Confucian religion did not prevent Chang from supporting his type of reform. But it was the concern he shared with K'ang to preserve China's traditional culture in general that was sufficient to override their doctrinal differences and to permit Chang to support K'ang's reform program.

The event that prompted Chang to change his stance from reform to revolution was the Boxer Uprising in 1900. This event proved that the Manchu government was incompetent to defend the nation. However, Chang's devotion to anti-Manchu revolution was mainly a means to preserve China's cultural heritage as evident in his identification of the study of national learning with the overthrow of the Manchu government.

As a revolutionary, Chang called for the preservation of the national essence. His emphasis on the national essence clearly distinguished him from most other revolutionaries, and placed him in a state of tension between political radicalism and cultural conservatism: which should be his priority, the preservation of the national essence or national survival? However, Chang's belief that the preservation of the national essence could strengthen the nation appeared to provide a resolution to this dilemma.

As a prominent revolutionary, Chang openly and bitterly attacked the Manchu government, and drew a distinct line between the Manchus and the Han Chinese race. As a result, Chang was regarded as an anti-Manchu racist and a Han chauvinist. This view, however, obscured the nature of Chang's thinking. Chang's anti-Manchuism was derived from his anti-imperialism, and was confined to his opposition to the Manchu government only. Thus, after the overthrow of the Manchu government, Chang no longer advocated anti-Manchuism.

Apart from his involvement in revolution, Chang promoted the national essence, which was a response to two major intellectual crisis of the time. One was Western impact; the other was K'ang's interpretation of Confucianism, which, in turn, exerted a great influence upon the New Culturists' attitude toward their own cultural tradition. The formation of Chang's concept of the national essence, however, owed a great deal to indigenous intellectual developments within China's late nineteenth century cultural legacy. In Confucianism, he saw the intellectual antidote to the sociomoral indifference of the School of Han Learning, which had dominated the mid-Ch'ing intellectual world.[10] Chang, probably the last great scholar of this school, however, upheld the teachings of Han Learning, which not only formed the foundation of his perceptions but encouraged him to widen his intellectual interests in many aspects of his tradition. Aside from Confucianism, the late nineteenth century witnessed a revival of interest in pre-Ch'in noncanonical texts and Mahayana Buddhism. All these three teachings have contributed important elements to Chang's concept of the national essence.

Chang's wide-raging intellectual interests also contributed to a variety of ideas that, when juxtaposed, appeared contradictory. However, in terms of his concern for the preservation of the national essence, much of this inconsistency was more apparent than real. For example, as a classical scholar, Chang denounced blanket acceptance of Confucianism because he thought that not all the elements in Confucianism were essential. Although Chang held that Confucianism had contributed significantly to the Chinese cultural tradition, he believed that the basic defect of Confucianism was the teaching to pursue wealth and high position. Thus, due to his concern for the preservation of the national essence, Chang

---

[10]Chang Hao, <u>Liang Ch'i-ch'ao</u>, pp. 14-15.

praised many essentials of Confucianism but criticized those elements he regarded as antithetical to this concept.

Chang's lifelong commitment to the preservation of the national essence manifested itself in his two careers: one as a classical scholar and the other as a political activist. Even after the founding of the republic and throughout the early 1930s, Chang remained active in the political arena. However, scholars held a view that after 1918 Chang withdrew almost completely from political activities. In fact, after 1918, Chang remained very active in the political arena rather than withdrawing from political activities. He was involved in the movement for the confederation of autonomous provinces in the 1920s and in the crusade against Japanese invasion in the 1930s.

Throughout his life, Chang was at the center of the political and intellectual arena. Before the founding of the republic, Chang was regarded as a radical anti-Manchu revolutionary. However, in early Republican Era, Chang was portrayed as a conservative for his involvement in the National Essence Movement, a culturally conservative movement, which arose as reaction against the rise of radical anti-traditionalism and wholesale westernization.

Scholars, then, argued over whether Chang was a radical or a conservative.[11] Some have concluded that Chang underwent an intellectual development from an

---

[11]Furth, "The Sage As Rebel", p. 114.

early period of radicalism to a later period of conservatism.[12] But his ideas did
not reflect a progression toward the latter. Although Chang can be described as
a political radical, he was also -- and consistently -- a conservative, or more
precisely a cultural conservative. However, it would be more accurate to say that
Chang was in essence a conservative, for the conservative element has been
present in his thinking in his early years and throughout his life.

Even during his careers as reformer, revolutionary, and political activist in
Republican China, Chang devoted himself to the promotion of the Chinese cultural
heritage. Chang's devotion to these political activities or radical politics was largely
a means to protect China's traditional culture threatened with extinction from
foreign powers, and to assure its continuity.

As a cultural conservative, Chang was not committed to the prevailing
republican political order; however, he had no objection to building China into a
modern nation.[13] Nevertheless, he maintained that a new China must be built
with reference to China's entire experience and history. In short, Chang did not
oppose structural and conceptual change or innovation in politics, but he favored
change with continuity.[14]

---

[12]Wong, <u>Search for Modern Nationalism</u>, p. ix.

[13]<u>Ibid</u>., p. viii.

[14]<u>Ibid</u>.

Upon the birth of the republic, most revolutionaries and constitutionalists favored the borrowing of American or French models for the new China; Chang objected to the uncritical wholesale transplantation of Western institutions or systems. He reminded them that China was not a newly created nation, thus, any change of political institutions must take its tradition into account.[15] Chang insisted that China should retain its cultural and institutional uniqueness, for without its cultural uniqueness, China could not maintain its national identity.[16] For Chang, China's cultural identity arose directly from its own essence. Thus, in terms of Chang's concern for the preservation of the national essence, Chang did not oppose change but maintained that any change should be within China's context.

---

[15]Sun, op. cit., pp. 61-62.

[16]Wong, Search for Modern Nationalism, p. viii.

SELECTED BIBLIOGRAPHY

Chinese Sources

Chang Nien-ch'ih 章念馳　　　　　　, ed., <u>Chang T'ai-yen sheng-p'ing yü hsüeh-shu</u> 章太炎生平與學術　　　　　　(Chang Ping-lin's Life and Scholarship), (Hong Kong: San-lien shu tien, 1988).

Chang Nien-ch'ih 章念馳　　　　　　, ed., <u>Chang T'ai-yen sheng-p'ing yü ssu-hsiang yen-chiu wen-hsüan</u> 章太炎生平與思想研究文選 (Selected Essays on Chang Ping-lin's Life and Thought), (Chekiang: Jen-min ch'u-pan she, 1986).

Chang P'eng-yüan 張朋園　　　　　, <u>Liang Ch'i-ch'ao yü Ch'ing-chi ke-ming</u> 梁啓超與清季革命　　　　　　(Liang Ch'i ch'ao and the Late Ch'ing Revolution), (Taipei: Chung-yang yen-chiu-yüan chin-tai-shih yen-chiu-so, 1964).

Chang Ping-lin 章炳麟　　　　　　　, <u>Chang T'ai-yen te pai-hua-wen</u> (The Vernacular Writings by Chang Ping-lin), (Taipei: I-wen yin-shu-kuan, 1972).

Chang Ping-lin 章炳麟　　　　　　, <u>Kuo-hsüeh lüeh-shuo</u> 國學略說 (A Brief Introduction to National Studies), (Hong Kong: Hong Kong huan-ch'iu wen-hua fu-wu she, 1963).

Chang Ping-lin 章炳麟　　　　　, <u>T'ai-yen hsien-sheng tzu-ting nien-p'u</u> 太炎先生自訂年譜(A Chronological Autobiography of Chang Ping-lin), (Taipei: Wen-hai ch'u-pan she, 1965).

Chang Ping-lin 章炳麟　　　　　　, "Wo te p'ing-sheng yü pan-shih fang-fa" 我的平生與辦事方法　　(My Life and Methods for Accomplishing Things) in <u>Chang T'ai-yen te pai-hua-wen</u> (The Vernacular Writings by Chang Ping-lin), (Taipei: I-wen yin-shu kuan, 1972), pp. 88-101.

<u>Chang-shih ts'ung-shu</u> 章氏叢書　　　　　, (The Collected Writings of Chang Ping-lin), 2 vols., (Taipei: Shih-chieh shu-chü, 1982).

Chang T'ai-yen ch'üan-chi　章太炎全集　　　　　, (The Complete Works of Chang Ping-lin), (Shanghai: Jen-min ch'u-pan she, 1982-6).

Chang Yin　張岱　　, "Ku-ching ching-she ch'u kao"　詁經精舍初稿 (Preliminary Draft of a Gazetteer of the Ku-ching ching-she), Wen-lan hsüeh-pao　文瀾學報　2:1 (March, 1936), pp. 1-47.

Chang Yü-fa　張玉法　　　, Ch'ing-chi te ke-ming t'uan-t'i　清季的革命團體 (Revolutionary Groups of the Late Ch'ing Period), Taipei: Chung-yang yen-chiu-yüan chin-tai-shih yen-chiu-so, 1982).

Cheng I-mei　鄭逸梅　　　, Nan-she ts'ung-t'an　南社叢談　　　(A Collected Record of Nan-she), (Shanghai: Jen-min ch'u-pan she, 1981).

Chiang I-hua　姜義華　　　and Chu Wei-cheng　朱維錚　　, eds., Chang T'ai-yen hsüan-chi　章太炎選集　　(Selected Works of Chang Ping-lin), (Shanghai: Jen-min ch'u-pan she, 1981).

Chiang I-hua　姜義華　　, Chang T'ai-yen ssu-hsiang yen-chiu　章太炎思想 研究　　(A Study of Chang Ping-lin's Thought), (Shanghai: Jen-min ch'u-pan she, 1985).

Ch'ien Mu　錢穆　　, Kuo-hsüeh kai-lun　國學概論　　(An Introduction to Classical Studies), (Taipei: Commercial Press, 1974).

Chou Hung-jan　周弘然　　　, ed., Chang T'ai-yen hsüan-chi　章太炎選集 (Selected Works of Chang Ping-lin), (Taipei: P'a-mi-erh shu-tien, 1979).

Chou Yü-t'ung　周予同　, Ching chin-ku-wen hsüeh　經今古文學　　(Study of the New and Ancient Text Classics), (Taipei: Commercial Press, 1967).

Chu Hsi-tsu　朱希祖　　　, "Pen-shih Chang T'ai-yen hsien-sheng k'ou-shou shao-nien shih-chi pi-chi"　本師章太炎口授少年事蹟筆記　　　(Notes on My Teacher Mr Chang Ping-lin's Reminiscences of His Early Years), Chih-yen　制言　, vol. 25 1936), pp. 1-3.

Chu Hung-yüan　朱浤源　　　, "Min-pao chung te Chang T'ai-yen" 民報中 的章太炎　　　(Chang Ping-lin in the Min-pao Period), Ta-lu tsa-chih 大陸雜誌 68:2 (February 15, 1984), pp. 64-93.

Chu Hung-yüan　朱浤源　　　, T'ung-meng hui te ke-ming li-lun　同盟會的
　　革命理論　(The Theory of Revolution by the Revolutionary Alliance),
　　(Taipei: Chung-yang yen-chiu-yüan chin-tai-shih yen-chiu so, 1985).

Chu Tsu-keng　朱祖耿, "Chi pen-shih Chang-Kung tzsu-shu chih-hsüeh chih
　　kung-fu yu chih-hsiang"記本師章公自述治學之功夫與志向(Notes to My Teacher
　　Chang Ping-lin's own Account of Scholarly Accomplishment and Goal),
　　Chih-yen　制言　25 (September 16, 1936), pp. 1-6.

Ch'u Ch'eng-po　褚成博　　　, ed., Kuang-hsü Yü-hang hsien-chih kao
　　光緒餘杭縣志稿　　　(Draft Gazetteer of Yü-hang County in the Kuang-
　　hsü Era), 4 Vols.

Ch'üan Han-sheng　全漢昇　, "Ch'ing-mo te `Hsi-hsüeh ch'u Chung-kuo'
　　shuo"　清末的西學出中國說　　　(On the Western Learning Originated
　　from China in the Last Years of the Ch'ing Dynasty in Li Ting-i,李定一 et al.,
　　Chung-kuo chin-tai-shih lun-ts'ung　中國近代史論叢　　　　　　(A
　　Collection of Essays on the Modern History of China), (Taipei: Chen-chung
　　shu-chü, 1966), Series 1, Vol. 5, pp. 216-258.

Fan Ming-li　范明禮　, "Ch'ing-mo tzu-ch'an chieh-chi kuo-ts'ui pai te chi-ke
　　wen-ti"清末資產階級國粹派的幾個問題 Hsin-hai ke-ming-shih ts'ung-k'an
　　Vol. 7, pp. 71-90.

Feng Tzu-yu　馮自由　　, Chung-hua min-kuo k'ai-kuo ch'ien ke-ming shih
　　中華民國開國前革命史(A History of the Revolution before the Founding of the
　　Republic of China), 2 Vols., (Shanghai: Ko-ming-shih p'ien-chi she, 1928).

Feng Tzu-yu　馮自由　, Ko-ming i-shih　革命逸史　　　(An Informal
　　History of the Revolution), 2 Vols., (Peking: Chung-hua shu-chü, 1979).

Ho Ch'eng-hsüan　何成軒　, Chang Ping-lin te che-hsüeh ssu-hsiang
　　章炳麟的哲學思想 (Chang Ping-lin's Philosophical Thought), (Hupei: Jen-
　　min ch'u-pan-she, 1987).

Hsiao I-shan　蕭一山　,Ch'ing-tai t'ung-shih　清代通史　　　(A General
　　History of the Ch'ing Dynasty), 5 Vols., (Taipei: Commercial Press, 1962).

Hsü Shou-shang　許壽裳　, Chang Ping-lin 章炳麟　(Nanking: Sheng-li
　　ch'u-pan kung-ssu, 1945).

Hu Han-min 胡漢民 "Hu Han-min tzu-chüan" 胡漢民自傳 (Autobiography of Hu Han-min) in <u>Ke-ming wen-hsien</u> 革命文獻 , 3 (1953), pp. 373-442.

Hu Sheng-wu 胡繩武 and Chin Ch'ung-chi 金沖及 , "Hsin-hai ke-ming shih-ch'i Chang Ping-lin te cheng-chih ssu-hsiang" 辛亥革命時期章炳麟的政治思想 (The Political Thought of Chang Ping-lin at the Time of the 1911 Revolution), <u>Li-shih yen-chiu</u> 歷史研究 No. 4 (1961), pp. 1-20.

Hu Shih 胡　適 , <u>Tai Tung-yüan te che-hsüeh</u> 戴東原的哲學 (Tai Chen's Philosophy), (Taipei: Commercial Press, 1967).

Huang Hung-shou 黃鴻壽 , <u>Ch'ing-shih chi-shih pen-mo</u> 清史紀事本末 (Topical History of the Ch'ing Dynasty), (Taipei: San-min shu-chü, 1959).

Kuo Chan-p'o 郭湛波 , <u>Chung-kuo chin-tai ssu-hsiang-shih</u> 中國近代思想史 (Modern Chinese Intellectual History), (Hong Kong: Lung-men shu-tien, 1965).

Li Chien-nung 李劍農 , <u>Tsui-chin san-shih-nien Chung-kuo cheng-chih-shih</u> 最近三十年中國政治史 (Chinese Political History in Recent Thirty Years), (Taipei: Hsueh-sheng shu-chü, 1976).

Liang Ch'i-ch'ao梁啓超, <u>Yin-ping-shih ch'üan-chi</u> 飲冰室全集 (The Complete Works of the Ice-Drinker's Studio), 48 vols., (Peking: Chung-hua chu-chü, n.d.).

Liang Hui-chin 梁惠錦 , "Nan-she: Ch'ing-mo Min-ch'u te ke-ming wen-i t'uan-t'i" 南社—清末民初的革命團體 (Nan-she: A Revolutionary and Literary Society in the Period of Late Ch'ing and Early Republic), <u>Chung-kuo li-shih hsüeh-hui shih-hsüeh chi-k'an</u> 中國歷史學會史學集刊 No. 12, pp. 247-261.

Liu Ya-tzu 柳亞子 , <u>Nan-she chi-lüeh</u> 南社紀略 (A Brief Record of Nan-she), (Taipei: Wen-hai ch'u-pan-she, n.d.).

Lu Hsün 魯迅 , "Kuan-yü T'ai-yen hsien-sheng erh-san-shih" 關於太炎先生二三事 (Few Things about Mr. Chang Ping-lin's Life and Scholarship) in Chang Nien-ch'ih 章念馳 , ed., <u>Chang T'ai-yen sheng-p'ing yü hsüeh shu</u> 章太炎生平與學術 (Hong Kong: San-lien shu-tien, 1988), pp. 8-10.

Lu Hsün 魯迅 , <u>Lu Hsün ch'üan-chi</u> 魯迅全集 (The Complete Works of Lu Hsün), 16 Vols., (Peking: Jen-min ch'u-pan she, 1981).

Lu Yüan-chün 盧元駿 , "Ching-hsüeh chi fa-chan yü chin-ku-wen chih fen- ho" 經學之發展與今古文之分合 (The Development of Classical Studies, and the Union and Division of the New and Ancient Text Classics) in Wang Ching-chih 王靜芝 , ed., <u>Ching-chüeh yen-chiu lun-chi</u> 經學研究論集 (Collected Essays on the Study of Classics), (Taipei: Li-ming ch'u-pan she, 1981), pp. 81-102.

Ma Tsung-huo 馬宗霍 , <u>Chung-kuo ching-hsüeh-shih</u> 中國經學史 (A History of Chinese Classical Studies), (Taipei: Commerical Press, 1979).

Ma Ying 馬瀛 , <u>Kuo-hsüeh kai-lun</u> 國學概論 (An Introduction to National Studies), (Taipei: Te-hua ch'u-pan she, 1978).

<u>Min-pao</u> 民報 (People's Journal), 8 Vols., (Taipei: Chung-kuo Kuo- min-tang chung-yang wei-yüan hui tang-shih shih-liao pien-tzuan wei-yüan hui, 1969).

P'i Hsi-jui 皮錫瑞 , <u>Ching-hsüeh li-shih</u> 經學歷史：史 (History of Classical Studies), (Taipei: I-wen yin-shu kuan, 1966).

Shen Sung-ch'iao 沈松僑 , <u>Hsüeh-heng-p'ai yü wu-ssu shih-ch'i te fan hsin-wen-hua-yün-tung</u> 學衡派與五四時期的反新文化運動 (The Critical Review Group: A Conservative Alternative to the New Culture Movement in the May Fourth Era), (Taipei: National Taiwan University Press, 1984).

Shen Yen-kuo 沈延國 , <u>Chi Chang T'ai-yen hsien-sheng</u> 記章太炎先生 (Remembering Mr. Chang Ping-lin), (Taipei: Wen-hai ch'u-pan she, n.d.).

Sung Chiao-jen 宋教仁 , Sung Chiao-jen jih-chi 宋教仁日記 (The Diary of Sung Chiao-jen), (Ch'ang-sha: Hunan jen-min ch'u-pan she, 1980).

Ta-Ch'ing li-ch'ao shih-lu 大清歷朝實錄 (Veritable Records through the Successive Reigns of the Ch'ing Dynasty), (Taipei: Hua-lien ch'u-pan she, 1964).

T'ang Chih-chün 湯志鈞 , Chang T'ai-yen cheng-lun hsüan-chi 章太炎政論選集 (Selected Political Essays of Chang Ping-lin), 2 vols., (Peking: Chung-hua shu-chü, 1977).

T'ang Chih-chün 湯志鈞 , ed., Chang T'ai-yen nien-p'u ch'ang-pien 章太炎年譜長編 (A Chronological Biography of Chang Ping-lin), 2 vols., (Peking: Chung-hua shu-chü, 1979).

T'ang Chih-chün 湯志鈞 , "Ch'ing-tai Ch'ang-chou ching chin-wen hsüeh-p'ai yü wu-hsü pien-fa 清代常州經今文派與戊戌變法 (The Ch'ing Dynasty New Text School in Ch'ang-chou and the 1898 Reform Movement) in T'ang Chih-chün, 湯志鈞 ed., Wu-hsü pien-fa-shih lun-ts'ung 戊戌變法史論叢 (A Collection of Essays on the Reform Movement of 1898), (Hong Kong: Ch'ung-wen shu-tien, 1973), pp. 71-81.

T'ang Chih-chün 湯志鈞 , "Ts'ung Ch'iu-shu te hsiu-ting k'an Chang T'ai-yen te ssu-hsiang yen-pien"從扈書的修訂看章太炎的思想演變(The Evolution of Chang Ping-lin's Thought as Reflected in the Different Editions of Ch'iu-shu), Wen-wu 文物 no. 11 (1975), pp. 59-74.

T'ang Wen-ch'üan 唐文權 and Lo Fu-hui 羅福惠 , Chang T'ai-yen ssu-hsiang yen-chiu 章太炎思想研究 (A Study of Chang Ping-lin's Thought), (Wu-ch'ang: Hua-chung shih-fan ta-hsüeh ch'u-pan she, 1986).

Ting Wen-chiang 丁文江 , Liang Jen-kung hsien-sheng nien-p'u ch'ang- pien ch'u-kao 梁任公先生年譜長編初稿 (Draft of a Chronological Biography of Liang Ch'i-ch'ao), 2 vols., (Taipei: Shih-chieh shu-chü, 1962).

Tsou Lu 鄒 魯 , Chung-kuo Kuo-min-tang shih-kao 中國國民黨史稿 (A Draft History of the Kuo-min-tang), (Ch'ang-sha: Commerical Press, 1938).

Tu Wei-yün 杜維運　, Hsüeh-shu yü shih-pien 學術與世變 (Scholarship and Epochal Change), (Taipei: Huan-yü ch'u-pan she, 1971).

Wang Ching-chih 王靜芝　, Ching-hsüeh t'ung-lun 經學通論 (General Discussions on Classical Studies), 2 vols., (Taipei: Kuo-li pien-i kuan, 1972).

Wang Erh-min 王爾敏 , Wan-Ch'ing cheng-chih ssu-hsiang-shih lun 晚清政治思想史論 (Historical Essays on Political Thought in the Late Ch'ing Period), (Taipei: Hsüeh-sheng shu-chü, 1969).

Wang Fan-sen 王汎森 , Chang T'ai-yen te ssu-hsiang, 1868-1919, 章太炎的思想 (The Thought of Chang Ping-lin), (Taipei: Shih-pao ch'u- pan she, 1985).

Wang Hsien-ch'ien 王先謙 , ed., Shih-i-ch'ao Tung-hua-lu 十一朝東華錄 (Notes from the Manchu Archives of the Eleven Reigns), (Shanghai: T'u-shu chi-ch'eng chen-pen chü, 1887).

Wang Tzu-ch'en 王淄塵 , Kuo-hsüeh chiang-hua 國學講話 (Discussions on National Studies), (Taipei: Hung-tao wen-huá shih-yeh yu-hsien kung-ssu, 1974).

Wang Yu-wei 王有爲 , Chang T'ai-yen chuan 章太炎傳 (A Biography of Chang Ping-lin), (Kuangtung: Jen-min ch'u-pan she, 1984).

Wang Yu-wei 王有爲 "P'ing Chang T'ai-yen te 'ke-ming-chün ch'i, ko-ming- tang hsiao'" 評章太炎的革命軍起，革命黨消 (A Review of Chang Ping-lin's "When the Revolutionary Army Arises, the Revolutionary Parties Should Be Abolished") in Chang Nien-ch'ih 章念馳 , ed., Chang T'ai-yen sheng-p'ing yü ssu-hsiang yen-chiu wen-hsuan 章太炎生平與思想研究文選 (Selected Essays on Chang Ping-lin's Life and Thought), (Chekiang: Jen-min ch'u-pan she, 1986).

Wong Young-tsu 汪榮祖 , "K'ang Yu-wei Chang Ping-lin ho-lun" 康有爲、章炳麟合論 , (A Study of K'ang Yu-wei and Chang Ping-lin), Chung-yang yen-chiu-yüan chin-tai-shih yen-chiu-so chi-k'an 中央研究院近代史研究所集刊 , v. 15, pt. 1, pp. 115-170.

Wu Hsiang-hsiang 吳相湘 , "Chang Ping-lin tzu-jen feng-tien" 章炳麟自認瘋顛 (Chang Ping-lin Admits Himself as a Madman), Chuan-chi wen-hsueh 傳記文學 42:4 (April, 1983), pp. 23-32.

Yang T'ien-shih 楊天石 , "Lun Hsin-hai ke-ming ch'ien te kuo-ts'ui chu-i ssu-ch'ao" 論辛亥革命前的國粹主義思潮 (On the Intellectual Movement for the Rejuvenation of the National Essence in the Years before the Revolution of 1911) in Chung-kuo chin san -pai-nien hsüeh-shu ssu-hsiang lun-chi 中國近三百年學術思想論集, v. 5, pp. 34-44.

Yang T'ien-shih 楊天石 and Liu Yen-ch'eng 劉彥成 , Nan-she 南社 (The Southern Society), (Peking: Chung-hua shu-chü, 1980).

Yüan Nai-ying 袁乃瑛 , "Yü-hang Chang-shih chih ching-hsüeh" 餘杭章氏之經學 , (The Classical Studies of Chang Ping-lin from Yü-hang County), Taiwan sheng-li shih-fan ta-hsüeh kuo-wen yen-chiu-so chi-k'an 臺灣省立師範大學國文研究所集刊(Taiwan . . .), no. 6 (June, 1962), pp. 219-258.

English Sources

Alitto, Guy S., The Last Confucian: Liang Shu-ming and the Chinese Dilemma of Modernity (Berkeley: University of California Press, 1979).

Ayers, William, Chang Chih-tung and the Educational Reform in China (Cambridge: Harvard University Press, 1971).

Bays, Daniel H., China Enters the Twentieth Century: Chang Chih-tung and the Issues of the New Age, 1895-1909 (Ann Arbor: The University of Michigan Press, 1978.

Bernal, Martin, Chinese Socialism to 1907 (Ithaca: Cornell University Press, 1976).

Bernal, Martin, "Liu Shih-p'ei and National Essence" in Charlotte Furth, ed., The Limits of Change: Essays on Conservative Alternatives in Republican China (Cambridge: Harvard University Press, 1976), pp. 90-112.

Bernal, Martin, "The Triumph of Anarchism over Marxism, 1906-1907" in Mary C. Wright, ed., China in Revolution: The First Phase, 1900-1913 (New Haven: Yale University Press, 1968), pp. 97-142.

Boorman, Howard L., and Howard, Richard, eds., Biographical Dictionary of Republican China, 4 vols. (New York: Columbia University Press, 1967).

Chan Sin-wai, Buddhism in Late Ch'ing Political Thought (Hong Kong: The Chinese University Press, 1985).

Chan Wing-tsit, A Source Book in Chinese Philosophy (Princeton: Princeton University Press, 1969).

Chan Wing-tsit, Chu Hsi: Life and Thought (Hong Kong: The Chinese University Press, 1987).

Chan Wing-tsit, "Chu Hsi's Completion of Neo-Confucianism" in Wing-tsit Chan, Chu Hsi: Life and Thought (Hong Kong: The Chinese University Press, 1987), pp. 103-138.

Chang Hao, Chinese Intellectuals in Crisis: Search for Order and Meaning (1890-1911) (Berkeley: University of California Press, 1987).

Chang Hao, "Intellectual Change and the Reform Movement, 1890-8" in Denis Twitchett and John K. Fairbank, eds., The Cambridge History of China (Cambridge: Cambridge University Press, 1980), vol. 11, pp. 274-338.

Chang Hao, Liang Ch'i-ch'ao and Intellectual Transition in China, 1890-1907 (Berkeley: University of California Press, 1971).

Chang P'eng-yüan, "The Constitutionists" in Mary C. Wright, ed., China in Revolution: The First Phase, 1900-1913 (New Haven: Yale University Press, 1973), pp. 143-183.

Chen Chi-yun, Hsün Yüeh (A.D. 148-209): The Life and Reflections of an Early Medieval Confucian (New York: Cambridge University Press, 1975).

Ch'eng Chung-ying, Tai Chen's Inquiry into Goodness (Honolulu: East-West Center Press, 1971).

Ch'ien Edward T., Chiao Hung and the Restructuring of Neo-Confucianism in the

Late Ming (New York: Columbia University Press, 1986).

Ch'ien Edward T., "Chiao Hung and the Revolt against Ch'eng-Chu Orthodoxy" in Wm. Theodore de Bary, ed., The Unfolding of Neo-Confucianism (New York: Columbia University Press, 1975), pp. 271-303.

Cohen, Paul A., Between Tradition and Modernity: Wang T'ao and Reform in Late Ch'ing China (Cambridge: Harvard University Press, 1974).

Chow Tse-tsung, "The Anti-Confucian Movement in Early Republican China" in Arthur F. Wright, ed., The Confucian Persuasion (Stanford: Stanford University Press, 1960), pp. 288-312.

Chow Tse-tsung, The May Fourth Movement: Intellectual Revolution in Modern China (Cambridge: Harvard University Press, 1960).

Chu Samuel C., Reformer in Modern China: Chang Chien, 1853-1926 (New York: Columbia University Press, 1965).

de Bary, Wm. Theodore, "A Reappraisal of Neo-Confucianism" in Arthur Wright, ed., Studies in Chinese Thought (Chicago: University of Chicago Press, 1953), pp. 81-111.

de Bary, Wm. Theodore, et al., Sources of Chinese Tradition (New York: Columbia University Press, 1961).

de Bary, Wm. Theodore, ed., The Unfolding of Neo-Confucianism (New York: Columbia University Press, 1975).

Duiker, William J., Ts'ai Yüan-p'ei: Educator of Modern China (Philadelphia: Pennsylvania University Press, 1977).

Dutt, Vidya Prakash, "The First Week of Revolution: The Wuchang Uprising" in Mary C. Wright, ed., China in Revolution: The First Phase, 1900-1913 (New Haven: Yale University Press, 1973), pp. 383-416.

Elman, Benjamin, From Philosophy to Philology (Cambridge: Harvard University Press, 1984).

212

Elman, Benjamin, "The Unravelling of Neo-Confucianism: The Lower Yangtze Academic Community in Late Imperial China" (Ph.D. Dissertation, University of Pennsylvania, 1980).

Fairbank, John K., East Asia: The Modern Transformation (Boston: Houghton Mifflin, 1965).

Fairbank, John K., and Denis Twitchett, eds., The Cambridge History of China, vol. 11 (Cambridge: Cambridge University Press, 1980).

Folsom, Kenneth E., Friends, Guests, and Colleagues: The Mu-fu System in the Late Ch'ing Period (Berkeley: University of California Press, 1968).

Fung, Yu-lan, A History of Chinese Philosophy, tr., Derk Bodde, 2 vols., (Princeton: Princeton University Press, 1953).

Furth, Charlotte, "Culture and Politics in Modern Chinese Conservatism" in Charlotte Furth, ed., The Limits of Change: Essays on Conservative Alternatives in Republican China (Cambridge: Harvard University Press, 1976), pp. 22-53.

Furth, Charlotte, ed., The Limits of Change: Essays on Conservative Alternatives in Republican China (Cambridge: Harvard University Press, 1976).

Furth, Charlotte, "The Sage as Rebel: The Inner World of Chang Ping-lin" in Charlotte Furth, ed., The Limits of Change: Essays on Conservative Alternatives in Republican China (Cambridge: Harvard University Press, 1976).

Gasster, Michael, Chinese Intellectuals and the Revolution of 1911: The Birth of Modern Chinese Radicalism (Seattle: University of Washington Press, 1968).

Gasster, Michael, "The Republican Revolutionary Movement" in Denis Twitchett and John K. Fairbank, eds., The Cambridge History of China, vol. 11 (Cambridge: Cambridge University Press, 1980), pp. 463-534.

Goodrich, Luther C., The Literary Inquisition of Ch'ien-lung (Baltimore: Waverly Press, 1935).

Grieder, Jerome B., Hu Shih and the Chinese Renaissance: Liberalism in the Chinese Revolution, 1917-1937 (Cambridge: Harvard University Press, 1970).

Haeger, John Winthrop, ed., Crisis and Prosperity in Sung China (Tucson: The University of Arizona Press, 1975).

Hao Yen-p'ing and Wang Erh-min, "Changing chinese Views of Western Relations, 1840-95" in Denis Twitchett and John K. Fairbank, eds., The Cambridge History of China, vol. 11 (Cambridge: Cambridge University Press, 1980), pp. 142-201.

Hatano, Yoshirhiro, "The New Armies" in Mary C. Wright, ed., China in Revolution: The First Phase, 1900-1913 (New Haven: Yale University Press, 1973), pp. 365-382.

Hedtke, Charles H., "The Szechwanese Railroad Protection Movement: Themes of Change and Conflict", Bulletin of the Institute of Modern History, v. 6 (June, 1977), pp. 355-407.

Hsiao, Kung-chuan, A Modern China and a New World: K'ang Yu-wei, Reformer and Utopian, 1858-1927 (Seattle: University of Washington Press, 1975).

Hsü Immanuel C. Y., "Late Ch'ing Foreign Relations, 1866-1905" in Denis Twitchett and John K. Fairbank, eds., The Cambridge History of China, vol. 11 (Cambridge: Cambridge University Press, 1980), pp. 70-141.

Hsü Immanuel C. Y., The Rise of Modern China (New York: Oxford University Press, 1975).

Hsüeh Chün-tu, Huang Hsing and the Chinese Revolution (Stanford: Stanford University Press, 1961).

Hu Sheng, et al., The 1911 Revolution: A Retrospective after 70 Years (Peking: New World Press, 1983).

Hucker, Charles O., ed., A Dictionary of Official Titles in Imperial China (Stanford: Stanford University Press, 1985).

Hummel, Arthur W., ed., Eminent Chinese of the Ch'ing Period (1644-1912), 2 vols. (Washington: Government Printing Office, 1943-44).

Jansen, Marius, "Japan and the Chinese Revolution of 1911" in Denis Twitchett and John K. Fairbank, eds., The Cambridge History of China, vol. 11 (Cambridge: Cambridge University Press, 1980), pp. 339-374.

Jones, Susan Mann, "Scholasticism and Politics in Late Eighteenth Century China" Ch'ing-shih wen-t'i 3:4 (December, 1975), pp. 28-49.

Kessler, Lawrence, "Chinese Scholars and the Early Manchu State" Harvard Journal of Asiatic Studies 31 (197), pp. 179-200.

Kracke, E. A., Jr., "Sung Society: Change within Tradition" Far Eastern Quarterly, v. 14 (1954-55), pp. 479-488.

Kuo, Thomas C., Chen Tu-hsiu (1879-1942) and the Chinese Communist Movement (New Jersey: Seton Hall University Press, 1975).

Lee, Feigon, Chen Duxiu: Founder of the Chinese Communist Party (Princeton: Princeton University Press, 1983).

Lee, Mabel, "Chang Ping-lin's Concept of Self and Society: Questions of Constancy and Continuity after the 1911 Revolution" in Conference on the Early History of China, 1917-1927 (Taipei: Chung-yang yen-chiu-yen chin-tai-shih yüan chiu so, 1984), v. 2, pp. 593-628.

Lee Ta-ling, Foundations of the Chinese Revolution, 1905-1912: An Historical Record of the T'ung-meng-hui (New York: St. Johns University Press, 1970).

Legge, James, tr., The Four Books (Taipei: Tun-huang shu-chü, n.d.).

Leung, Man-kam, "Chang Ping-lin: His Life and Career", Lien-ho shu-yüan hsüeh-pao, no. 8 (1970), pp. 97-108.

Levenson, Joseph R., Confucian China and Its Modern Fate, 3 vols., (Berkeley: University of California Press, 1965).

Li, "Zhang Taiyan as a Revolutionary and a Thinker" in The 1911 Revolution: A Retrospective after 70 Years (Peking: New World Press, 1983), pp. 183-202.

Liang Ch'i-ch'ao, Intellectual Trends in the Ch'ing Period, tr. Immanuel C. Y. Hsü (Cambridge: Harvard University Press, 1959).

Liu, James T. C., Ou-yang Hsiu: An Eleventh-Century Neo-Confucianist (Stanford: Stanford University Press, 1967).

Liu, Wang Hui-chen, "An Analysis of Chinese Clan Rules: Confucian Theories in Action" in David S. Nivison and Arthur F. Wright, eds., Confucianism in Action (Stanford: Stanford University Press, 1959).

Lo, Winston W., "Philology, an Aspect of Sung Rationalism", Chinese Culture, 17:4 (December, 1976), pp. 1-26.

Nivison, David S. and Wright, Arthur F., eds., Confucianism in Action (Stanford: Stanford University Press, 1959).

Onions, C. T., ed., The Oxford Universal Dictionary of Historical Principles (Oxford: Oxford University Press, 1955).

Pulleyblank, Edwin, "Neo-Confucianism and Neo-Legalism in T'ang Intellectual Life, 755-805" in Arthur Wright, ed., The Confucian Persuasion (Stanford: Stanford University Press, 1960), pp. 77-114.

Pyle, Kenneth B., The New Generation in Meiji Japan: Problems of Cultural Identity, 1885-1895 (Stanford: Stanford University Press, 1969).

Rankin, Mary Backus, Early Chinese Revolutionaries: Radical Intellectuals in Shanghai and Chekiang, 1902-1911 (Cambridge: Harvard University Press, 1971).

Rosen, Richard Barry, "The National Heritage Opposition to the New Culture and Literary Movements of China in the 1920's" (Ph.D. Dissertation, University of California, Berkeley, 1969).

Schiffrin, Harold Z., Sun Yat-sen and the Origins of the Chinese Revolution (Berkeley: University of California Press, 1968).

Schneider, Laurence A., Ku Chieh-kang and China's New History: Nationalism and the Quest for Alternative Traditions (Berkeley: University of California Press, 1971).

Schneider, Laurence A., "National Essence and the New Intelligentsia" in Charlotte Furth, ed., The Limits of Change: Essays on Conservative Alternatives in Republican China (Cambridge: Harvard University Press, 1976), pp. 57-89.

Schwartz, Benjamin I., "Notes on Conservatism in General and in China in Particular" in Charlotte Furth, ed., The Limits of Change: Essays on Conservative Alternatives in Republican China (Cambridge: Harvard University Press, 1976), pp. 3-22.

Sheridan, James E., China in Disintegration: The Republican Era in Chinese History, 1912-1949 (New York: The Free Press, 1975).

Shiba, Yoshinobu, "Urbanization and the Development of Markets in the Lower Yangtze Valley" in John Winthrop Haeger, ed., Crisis and Prosperity in Sung China (Tucson: The University of Arizona Press, 1975), pp. 13-48.

Som Tjan Tjoe, Po-hu-t'ung, 2 vols., (Leiden: E. J. Brill, 1949).

Sun Warren, "Chang Ping-lin and his Political Thought" Paper on Far Eastern History (September, 1985), pp. 57-69.

Teng Ssu-yü, et al., China's Response to the West: A Documentary Survey, 1839-1923 (Cambridge:Harvard University Press, 1954).

Twitchett, Denis, "The Fan Clan's Charitable Estate, 1050-1760" in David S. Nivison and Arthur F. Wright, eds., Confucianism in Action (Stanford: Stanford University Press, 1959).

Wang Y. C., "The Su-pao Case: A Study of Foreign Pressure, Intellectual Fermentation, and Dynastic Decline", Monumenta Serica, vol. 24 (1965), pp. 84-129.

Welch, Holmes, The Buddhist Revival in China (Cambridge, Harvard University Press, 1968).

Wiener, Philip P., ed., Dictionary of the History of Ideas, 5 vols., (New York: Charles Scribner's Sons, 1973).

Wilhelm, Hellmut, "The Po-hsüeh Hung-ju Examination of 1679" Journal of the American Oriental Society, 71 (1951), pp. 60-66.

Wong Young-tzu, Search for Modern Nationalism: Zhang Binglin and Revolutionary China, 1869-1936 (Oxford: Oxford University Press, 1989).

Wright, Mary C., ed., China in Revolution: The First Phase, 1900-1913 (New Haven: Yale University Press, 1968).

Wright, Mary C., "Introduction: The Rising Tide of Change" in Mary C. Wright, ed., China in Revolution: The First Phase, 1900-1913 (New Haven: Yale University Press, 1973), pp. 1-63.

Wright, Arthur, ed., Studies in Chinese Thought (Chicago: University of Chicago Press, 1953).

Wright, Arthur F., ed., The Confucian Persuasion (Stanford: Stanford University Press, 1960).

Young, Ernest P., The Presidency of Yüan Shih-K'ai: Liberalism and Dictatorship in Early Republican China (Ann Arbor: University of Michigan Press, 1977).

Yü Ying-shih, "Some Preliminary Observations on the Rise of Ch'ing Confucian Intellectualism" Tsing Hua Journal of Chinese Studies, 11 (1975), pp. 105-146.